The Puppet Book

The Puppet Book

*How to Make and Operate Puppets
and Stage a Puppet Play*

by CLAIRE BUCHWALD

Illustrations by Audrey Jakubiszyn

Publishers   PLAYS, INC.   *Boston*

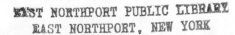

Library of Congress Cataloging-in-Publication Data

Buchwald, Claire.
  The puppet book : how to make and operate puppets and stage a
puppet play / by Claire Buchwald ; illustrated by Audrey Jakubiszyn.
    p. cm.
  Includes bibliographical references.
  Summary: Presents instructions for making a puppet stage, hand
puppets, sets and props, and a pre-recorded soundtrack of a play;
provides tips on rehearsing and performing a puppet play; and
includes six original plays.
  ISBN 0-8238-0293-0
  1. Puppet theater. 2. Puppets. [1. Puppets. 2. Puppet plays.
3. Plays.] I. Jakubiszyn, Audrey, ill. II. Title.
PN1970.B87 1990
791.5′3—dc20   90-38080
                                            CIP
                                            AC

Manufactured in the United States of America

◆◆ *Contents* ◆◆

Part I: The Puppet Theater

Part II: The Plays

This book is dedicated with love to

my Opa
for his stories, his humor,
and his gift for the practical

and to

my parents
who have shown me the potential of effort and imagination

Acknowledgments

I gained the experience that inspired my interest in puppetry from my work with the unique traveling puppet wagon of Edina, Minnesota.

I am indebted to the Park and Recreation Department of the City of Edina. I am grateful to those early puppeteers and city staff who built the puppet wagon and developed the techniques that were passed on to me. I also would like to thank the resourceful and talented puppeteers whom I was privileged to work with: Larry Bogoslaw, Mary Malecki, Shannon Murphy, and Lynne Peissig.

Among others who assisted us were Amy Buchwald, Charles Lukaszewski, and Katy Schackor. The wonderful staffs of the Edina Public Library and Minnesota Fabrics (Southtown) were of great help. A smile, too, to the appreciative Edina audiences who made our work worthwhile.

I would not have been able to write this book without the loving and multi-faceted support of my parents.

I am grateful to Larry Bogoslaw, who painstakingly edited every page of the manuscript, and who works constant magic in my life.

As always, Dorothy Clingingsmith provided technical assistance and confidence.

The encouragement of Barbara Esbensen has meant a great deal to me.

Working with Audrey Jakubiszyn has been a joy and an honor.

Finally, I gratefully acknowledge Sylvia Burack, who was willing to publish a new author, and Elizabeth Preston, who wrestled with the final editing of *The Puppet Book*.

Preface

The Puppet Book grew out of two summers' experience working as a puppeteer for the city of Edina, Minnesota. Both summers, I wrote the scripts for the puppet plays. I was one of three people responsible for all aspects of puppet show production: making the stage properties and sets, pre-recording a soundtrack of each play, keeping an aging puppet wagon in repair, and driving to fifteen parks each week to perform the shows for children, camp counselors, and parents.

The Edina Puppet Wagon has been popular summer entertainment since the early 1960s. During the summers of 1986 and 1988, we received many compliments from parents that ours were among the best shows they had seen. We felt proud of our shows because we put a great deal of thought and care into them. It was my intention to write plays that adults, as well as children, would enjoy. Without losing sight of the play's crucial function as a form of entertainment, I tried to convey moral or social messages clearly. I also took care not to leave loose ends in my stories. Children are intelligent, and they deserve careful writing. Finally, I tried to push our resources and stage set-up to their limits, so that our audiences would have new and exciting surprises in each show.

For this book, I selected six puppet shows from my two seasons with the Puppet Wagon. I have rewritten them with the memory of performing them still in mind. I have provided only those stage directions and suggested only those stage properties which I know from experience to be feasible and worthwhile. Furthermore, the plots and language I use are accessible to American children of the 1990s; at the same time, they put less emphasis on weaponry and more on friendship, creativity, and perseverance than many current children's products.

I have written the book to be accessible to adults who wish to perform puppet shows for children, as well as groups of children from the middle grades and up, working under adult supervision.

This book will show you how to get started. Then, your own imaginations can take over.

CLAIRE BUCHWALD

PART I
The Puppet Theater

❦ 1 The Puppet Stage

Workable stages vary quite a bit depending on the time, materials, and expertise available to you. For the plays in this book, I suggest one of two simple stages. The first is a large enclosed box, built out of wood or some other strong material. Ideally, the dimensions should be six feet high by six feet long by five feet deep. (Diagram I.1)

An even simpler way to make a puppet stage is to use a large screen made of the thickest, sturdiest material possible; if using cardboard, make sure that it is firmly attached to the floor or other surface immediately beneath it. It should not wobble when touched by someone backstage and should be in no danger of falling over during the performance. Heavy boxes, like shipping boxes or large appliance boxes, will work well if they are properly secured. Open out the box and cut off the top and bottom pieces. You will be left with a long sheet of cardboard in four sections. (Diagram I.2)

Whether you use a box or a screen, the most important characteristics of your stage are a large central window and at least one small window on either side of it. All three windows should be at an appropriate height so that the puppeteers can sit on a bench beneath the center window and stand behind the side windows to operate the puppets. There should be a small, equal amount of space between the central window and each of two side windows. Suggested measurements: main window—3′ to 3′ 6″ wide by 2′ to 2′ 6″ high; side windows—one foot square. The height below the bottom of the main window should be at least three feet and no more than four feet. (Diagram I.3)

You may use the screen to section off part of a narrow room, allowing you to use all the space behind the screen as the backstage area. (Diagram I.4) You may also use the screen for the front face of the stage and use other screens or large objects to hide the backstage area from the sides—desks or tables placed on end, the legs extending outward, or sheets hanging from the ceiling, for instance. (Diagram I.5) As the diagram shows, it is not necessary for the screen you use for the front of the stage to cover the entire area from the ground to above the stage. Securely attach the screen—out of which you have cut the main window and side windows—on top of the edge of the desk or table. You may even cut the main window at the bottom of the screen so that it meets the top edge of the desk. Doing this will make performing most plays easier, because nails can be pounded into the bottom of the desk to support props from beneath. (Diagram I.6)

There should be enough room inside the box or behind the screen to allow puppeteers to move about easily, and to place all their puppets, sets, stage properties, and possibly a tape recorder, out of sight of the audience. Although the puppet shows in this book are designed with only two side windows in mind, you are by no means limited to this number—additional windows may be placed on either side of the central window, at various heights. They are effective in chase and hiding scenes, or when used to represent basements or tower windows. If you place additional windows too much lower than the other windows, however, they will be difficult for the puppeteer to work with and difficult for the audience to see clearly.

The curtain

The main window of your puppet stage will need a curtain that can be quickly opened or closed from backstage. If the screen or other piece used for the front of the stage is not sturdy enough to have a curtain attached to it, you can hang curtains on a rod or clothesline stretched between two objects (such as desks on end) on either side of the stage.

Inexpensive blinds can be found at hardware and discount department stores. A blind that closes from above by means of pullcords on one side works very well for a stage curtain, as do ready-made curtains, complete with rods and curtain assembly. If you wish to make your own curtain, I suggest using velvet or another thick material. Here are two of the simpler methods for making a curtain, and a pulley assembly to open and close it.

Straight curtain

Cut two pieces of fabric, each three to four inches taller than the main stage and slightly wider than half its width. Make several small reinforced holes along the top edge of each piece, and attach curtain rings through the holes.

The next step is to make a pullcord assembly. If stage windows are cut out of wood or very sturdy corrugated cardboard, you can attach the pullcord directly to the edges of the main window. (If the stage windows are cut from less sturdy material, you will want to attach the assembly to walls, desks set on end, or other supports on either side of the screen.)

Cut a strong piece of string or nylon cord about three times the width of the main stage, or three times the distance between strong supports. Buy three screw eyes from a hardware store, and attach two of them, with the heads facing backstage, on the right side of the main window, or on the right side support. The two should be attached one above the other, three inches apart, with the lower screw eye placed slightly higher than the top of the main window. Attach the third screw eye on the left side of the window, or left side support, level with the top screw eye on the right side. (Diagram I.7)

You will now thread the nylon cord through the screw eyes and curtain rings. Begin by sliding the cord through the upper of the two screw eyes on the right. Next, thread the cord through the rings of one curtain. Bring the cord to the left and thread it through the screw eye on that side of the stage. Now, bring the cord back to the right, sliding it through the rings of the other curtain. Finally, thread the cord through the lower screw eye on the right. You should now have two ends of the cord hanging down on the right side, one from the upper screw eye and one from the lower. (Diagram I.8) You will need to weight each end with a heavy tassel or large nut so that the cords will remain taut.

Spread out the curtain halves, making the piece on the upper length of cord the right half of the stage curtain and the piece on the lower length of the cord the left half. Secure the position of the curtain halves by tying the innermost curtain rings to the cord. Also, fastening the top corners of the curtain with staples or strong glue to the inside front of the stage will keep them in place when the curtain is opened and closed. To close the curtain, pull on the end of the cord that hangs from the upper screw eye; to open it, pull on the other end of the cord.

Drop curtain

If you are using a very sturdy stage—a box stage or a screen made from wood—you may choose to make a drop curtain, which can be lowered and raised on the stage window.

Cut a cloth rectangle approximately one inch wider and three inches taller than the main stage window. Sew three vertical rows of curtain rings on the back of the curtain, spaced evenly. The topmost ring should be approximately six inches from the top of the curtain. (Diagram I.9)

Using strong staples or nails, attach the top three inches of the curtain to the part of the stage above the window. If you prefer, you can wind the top three inches of fabric around a rod, then attach the rod above the stage on picture hooks placed on either side of the stage. Secure the rod to the hooks with strong rubber bands.

Attach three screw eyes above the curtain in line with each vertical row of curtain rings. The screw eye on the far left should be just above the top of the curtain; the next one to the right should be one inch higher; and the third, one inch higher than the second.

Attach a large screw eye a few inches to the left of the stage window, at the height of the highest screw eye. (Diagram I.10)

Cut three lengths of nylon cord: the shortest two and one half times the height of the curtain, and each successive cord a foot longer than the last.

Thread the shortest cord through the set of curtain rings on the far left, tying the cord to the bottommost ring. Now thread it through the screw eye above the row of rings, and from there, through the large screw eye to the left of the stage. Follow the same pattern with the other lengths of cord and rows of curtain rings, eventually threading all of the cords through the large screw eye to the left of the stage.

Tie all three lengths of cord together at the ends where they hang down from the large screw eye. Attach a weight to keep the cords taut. On the left side of the stage, near the bottom of the window, fasten a hook. Attach a metal or rope loop to the weight at the end of the cord. The loop should fit onto the hook to hold the curtain open. (Diagram I.11) When you pull on the cord, the whole curtain should rise from the bottom. To keep the curtain open, fit the loop onto the hook; to close the curtain, simply detach the loop from the hook.

The backdrop

A backdrop is a vertical flat surface in front of which sets are hung for performances. The backdrop should be placed about a foot behind the main stage window, and must be sturdy enough to support the weight of the sets.

You can make a backdrop by attaching a metal or wood bar from one side of the backstage area to another; from the top of the puppet theater (if it is an enclosed box stage); or from the ceiling of the room in which you are performing. (Diagram I.12) On this bar, you may hang a black cloth, over which you will hang your sets.

Portable blackboards, adjustable easels, collapsible screens, or similar objects also work well as backdrops, as long as they are strong enough to hold the sets. Simply place the easel or blackboard about a foot behind the puppet stage. You must consider that the puppeteer will be very close to the backdrop, essentially under and behind it, with part of his or her body between the backdrop and the stage window. Therefore, it is best if the backdrop extends just below the bottom of the puppet window, but no lower, except for legs or other supports. (Diagram I.13)

You should also attach black cloth behind the side windows, to hide the puppeteer. Staple or hammer the cloth into place on either side of each window, leaving the top and bottom unfastened. Do not stretch the cloth taut. The extra room will allow the puppeteer to place his hand and arm in front of the cloth when operating a puppet. (Diagram I.14)

Shelves and benches

The puppeteers need a bench or other sturdy surface to sit on when they are operating puppets in the main stage. The bench should be approximately the same length as the main window, and 15 to 18 inches high. You may also use a footlocker or sturdy box, or line up a few small chairs with their backs against the below-stage area. Tie the legs together so the chairs do not move apart during the performance. (Diagram I.15)

You will also need a large shelf or table to hold the puppets and props when not in use, and a tape recorder, if speakers placed in front of the stage are being used to carry the sound to the audience.

Small shelves placed just below the side windows backstage are useful for keeping props close at hand. (Diagram I.16) You may wish to make a triangular shelf to fit in the corners, or simply place a tall narrow box on end. If you do use a box, be sure to attach it to some part of the stage or fill it with something heavy to keep it from falling over during the play.

When not in use, sets may be propped up against a wall or table, stacked on the floor, or held in a magazine rack or easel.

❧❧ 2 Puppets

The plays in this book, as well as the stage described in the preceding chapter, are designed primarily for hand puppets, rather than marionettes. Hand puppets are simple to make, to use, and to change for a new play, and they are also the most versatile and expressive of non-string puppets. You should, however, feel free to experiment with rod and other puppets as well. In the production notes for each play in this book, there are suggestions for which kind of puppet I think will work best for each character.

Toy and gift stores carry many well-made animal hand puppets, as do some libraries; these puppets are ready to use, but you may have to make and attach an additional tube of fabric at the bottom to hide the puppeteer's entire forearm. (Diagram I.17)

Of course, it is always fun and rewarding to make your own puppets, and instructions for making various kinds of hand puppets follow.

Sock and oven-mitt puppets

For a snake, lizard, insect, fish, or similar puppet that does not need movable arms or legs, you may use a sock or, better still, a long oven mitt (available in kitchen supply stores). Use the kind of oven mitt with equally sized upper and lower jaws. You can put a felt tongue and fangs or teeth in the mouth, paste on eyes, and decorate the body appropriately. To help the mouth keep its shape, you may want to line the inside with a stiffer cloth or two lightweight pieces of cardboard. A paper plate cut to the right shape works well. Remember that whenever you are attaching anything to cloth, you will have much greater success with fabric or tacky glue than with multi-purpose glue.

For a puppet that needs movable arms, you may use a sock (but such a puppet will not have a movable mouth). There are two ways to make arms for sock puppets. The first is to cut and sew two rounded "arms" out of cloth that matches the material from which the puppet is made (if it is a sock puppet, you can use the sock's mate). Cut holes in the sock, reinforce the holes with stitching, and sew the arms in place. Hands may be cut out of felt and glued to the ends of the arms. (Diagram I.18)

A simpler method is to use an old glove. Cut holes in the sock the size of the thumb and little finger of the glove. Reinforce the holes securely by stitching around the perimeter of each several times with strong thread. (A good stitch to use is the blanket stitch.) When it is time to use the puppet, the puppeteer will place his hand first into the glove and then into the puppet, sticking his thumb out one of the holes and his little finger out the other for the puppet's arms. The middle three fingers will work together to operate the head. (Diagram I.19)

If the puppeteer's hand gets too hot using this method, or if it is too confining, the middle fingers of the glove can be cut off, or the two fingers of the glove used for arms can be cut off and sewn directly onto the puppet's body, covering each hole. Hands can be cut out of felt and glued to the ends of the arms.

Glove puppets

Glove puppets work well for monsters, trees, and bushes. To make a glove puppet, simply take a work glove and attach a tube of fabric at the base, to hide the puppeteer's arm. The tube should be joined with the glove on the inside so that stitching does not show. Eyes may be placed near the top of the palm of the glove, or all over, if it is a many-eyed monster. You may decorate the fingers and other parts of the glove puppet, if you wish. (Diagram I.20)

Puppets with papier-mâché heads and cloth bodies

To make puppets that look like people, I suggest making hand puppets with papier-mâché heads and cloth bodies.

Making papier-mâché heads

The simplest way to make a papier-mâché head is to use "instant papier-mâché," available in craft stores and some office supply stores. When

10

mixed with water, instant papier-mâché becomes a modeling clay-like material out of which you can form a head of any shape. To hold the shape of the head at the beginning and to insure that you leave a hollow neck so that the puppet can be operated, form the head on the top of an empty toilet paper roll. (Diagram I.21) Allow the papier-mâché to dry completely, then remove the cardboard tube, if possible. It is likely that the end of it will be stuck to the papier-mâché, in which case, simply cut away all of the roll beneath the neck.

Painting the face

Choose the color of skin you want for your puppet, and mix paints to make the hue. Paint the whole head this color, and allow it to dry. When it is completely dry, you can use paints of other colors for the eyes and mouth, and, if desired, dimples, freckles, or scars. You can also use dark paint or a shade of paint just a little darker than the color of the skin for wrinkles, the inside of ears, and nostrils. For rosy cheeks, add a rosy tint to the same paint you used for the skin.

When you have finished painting your puppet's face and allowed it to dry, spray it with a clear varnish to protect the paint and add luster.

Hair

Choose yarn for the puppet's hair, paying attention to the thickness as well as to the color. It is best to attach hair with a staple gun or strong glue—I prefer glue, because staples may be visible, depending on hair color and style.

First, cut the amount of yarn you will need to make the hair. You should glue down the yarn in two to four sections: In each section, first apply the glue, then the yarn. Press the yarn onto the glue and hold it in place for some time before moving to the next section. Usually, all the hair will spread outward from the center. (Diagram I.22)

If you are making a puppet with braids or a ponytail, you may paste one section of horizontal strips of yarn to the back of the head and then have two other long sections of hair falling vertically from a central part past the puppet's shoulders on either side. Arrange each long piece of yarn in a tight zigzag, starting from a part running along the center of the head, going down the side past the shoulders, up again, down again, etc. Glue the top few inches of this folded length of yarn securely to the head, stopping just above the ear. Cut the ends at the bottom to make individual hairs. Now, you may braid them or tie them on either side with bows. (Diagram I.23)

For a bun, spiral the hair from the center going outward, attaching it firmly against the head. Make a little knot of yarn for the bun itself and glue it on top of the other yarn.

When the head is complete, it is ready to be attached to a body. For each new show, you can reuse heads, repainting them and attaching them to new bodies if you wish.

Cloth bodies and costumes

The body and costume of the puppet are one and the same. You may use the dimensions suggested in Diagram I.24 as a guide. Cut out two identical pieces of fabric for the front and back of the puppet's body and arms. (If you wish, you can make the bottom of the puppet in cloth different from the top to give the impression of a two-piece outfit, as shown in Diagram I.25.) You should make the arms wide for the puppet's size, because once the front and back are sewn together, there must be plenty of room for the puppeteer's fingers inside.

Sew the pieces together inside out, so the stitching does not show when turned right side out. Place right sides together, and begin sewing, leaving the top and bottom edges open. The puppet's head will be attached to the top, and the puppeteer's hand will come up through the bottom. Make the stitches as close together as possible, and use strong thread of a color that matches the fabric. (Diagram I.26) When you are finished, turn the cloth body right side out.

Cut hands out of felt that is similar in color to the face. Glue them to the tips of the arms. Make sure they are not too big; if they flap around awkwardly when the puppet is moving its arms, you should trim them.

You may want to add more "clothing" to the body—for instance, a jacket or skirt made out of cloth, and glued or sewn to the body. It is best not to pile too many layers of clothes onto the body, because it will increase its size and weight, and may make it difficult for the puppeteer to use.

Imagination—not tremendous skill—is the key to clothing a puppet. It is not necessary to make a complete wardrobe of shirt, belt, and pair of overalls, and then try to put them on the puppet. For instance, if the lower part of the body is made of cloth different from the upper part, you need only glue on a strip of felt for a belt, and a small square of different-color felt for the belt buckle. Overalls can be made by gluing two strips of cloth from the waist, over the shoulder, to the waist in the back. Two or three small buttons cut out of felt and glued to the front of the cloth body will make it look as though the puppet is wearing a button-down shirt. One factor that greatly simplifies the making of costumes is that your puppet does not have legs; therefore, two pieces of fabric stitched together into a tube and attached to the puppet at the waist may be used to represent a skirt or pants. Keeping your designs simple, you can make dresses, jackets, coats, robes, overalls, or any other costume you wish.

Attaching the head to the body

Use strong glue or a staple gun to attach the body of the puppet to the head. If you use a staple gun, you should check carefully for loose staples before anyone puts the puppet on his or her hand.

Once the body is glued or stapled to the head, you can operate the head with your pointer and middle finger, the right hand with your two small fingers, and the left hand with your thumb. (Diagram I.27)

Remember: There is no right or wrong way to make a puppet, as long as it looks and works the way you want it to.

✦✦ 3 Sets and Props

Every puppet show needs sets—pictures that hang in the background and set the scene for the puppets' action. A set may be a kitchen, a dungeon, a field in front of a castle, a valley between mountains, a forest, the front yard of a cottage, a coral reef in the ocean, or anywhere else one can imagine.

Making sets

There are many ways to create scenery, but for the plays in this book, I suggest using large pieces of colored posterboard. Depending on the size of your stage, you may need to attach two pieces of posterboard together. The set does not always have to be drawn on a white background—yellow, orange, light blue, red, pale green, gray, and sometimes even black posterboard work very well.

Once you have chosen the posterboard, use paints and permanent markers to create a picture of the background. If you wish, you may paste smaller pieces of paper or cardboard or other items to the set. For example, you may want to paste little eyes (cut out of construction paper or bought at a craft store) onto black posterboard to depict a spooky, dark place.

You can cut an arch-shaped hole anywhere along the bottom of your set where you want a puppet to appear from the middle of the surroundings. For example, if a lion is supposed to come out of a cave, the puppet can be hiding behind the set, and then suddenly appear in the cut-out entrance to the cave. (Diagram I.28)

Remember that if you are using a straight curtain, the only part of the set visible to the whole audience will be the middle, so you will want to

14

concentrate most of the scenery in the center of the set. Make your sets as colorful, interesting, and attractive as possible.

Hanging sets

If you are using one of the puppet stages described in this book, you may prepare to hang your sets on the backdrop as follows. Place each set face down on a table. Pull a hanger into a square, as shown in Diagram I.29, and lay it on one half of the set. Pull another hanger into a square, and lay it on the other half of the set. Now, using masking tape, tape the hangers to the set as shown, using long pieces to tape down opposing corners and short pieces to reinforce each corner. You are now ready to hang the sets on your backdrop.

Open the curtain and step out in front of the theater to see how each set looks. Make the adjustments necessary so that each hangs straight and centered, and looks best from the place where your audience will be seated. For instance, if the audience will be sitting on the ground, sit on the ground yourself to check the appearance of the set from that level.

Stage properties

Stage properties, or "props," are helpful tools that can enhance your plays. Props are objects held or used by a character: a bag, magic wand, guitar, spaceship, television set, or table. Using your imagination and simple craft materials—scraps of cloth, construction paper, paints, colored markers, posterboard, aluminum foil, glitter, string, yarn, wire or pipe cleaners, tacky glue and multi-purpose glue—you can make props easily.

I recommend cutting props out of white posterboard or cardboard. You may also try to use construction paper, but it tends to crumple. I also suggest using permanent markers rather than paints to decorate props, since paint can flake or bend a prop.

Supporting a prop

A prop can be hung from above the stage, attached to a puppet with Velcro, or most commonly, held on a stick from below so that it appears to be resting on the stage. For sticks, you may use paint brushes, pencils, dowel rods, or twigs taped onto the back of the prop. Leave extra space between the bottom of the visible part of the prop and the place where the dowel sticks out. You do not want to spoil the illusion of the prop onstage by allowing the dowel to show. (Diagram I.30)

You can also make a prop that can be carried in and out on a stick during an act, yet also remain on stage for some time without being held from below. Make the prop and attach the rod to it. Then, if your stage allows, hammer large-headed nails or insert thumb tacks below the stage on the inside, but be sure they don't poke through on the outside. Put the nails or tacks just far enough in so that the bottom of the posterboard prop can rest on them. (Diagram I.31)

If your puppet stage has a wide enough bottom edge on which props may rest, you can sew or glue Velcro onto some props and onto the stage itself. Glue one piece of Velcro to the bottom edge of the stage where you want the prop to stand. Then, glue the corresponding piece to the bottom of the prop. Make sure the pieces are glued securely. (Diagram I.32) This technique works best when the props are going to remain in the same place onstage throughout the scene.

More often, you will use Velcro to allow puppets to "hold" lightweight props, such as swords or musical instruments. Sew one piece of Velcro onto the arm or hand of the puppet. Sew or glue a corresponding piece onto the prop. When it is time for a puppet to hold the prop, the puppeteer can attach it while the puppet is backstage. If the prop is too large or heavy, have the puppet hold it in his "arms"—that is, between the puppeteer's fingers. (Diagram I.33) Additional pieces of Velcro, or a string holding a prop around a puppet's neck, can provide even more support.

•• 4 The Sound Track

Although it is possible to work a puppet and speak its lines at the same time, there are many advantages to making a sound recording of the show before the actual performance. The main benefit is that during the performance, the puppeteers do not have to remember lines or create background noises while working the puppets and attending to the sets, curtains, and props. This results in a more polished performance, and easily allows for multiple performances of the same show. A recording can even be saved for use by other puppeteers.

All the shows in this book include music, and are designed to be pre-taped. Running time is between 10 and 20 minutes. Stage directions and production notes give suggestions for where music would be appropriate; of course, you may add music anywhere else you like.

Creating the sound track is a three-part job. First, you will select the music you want for the show, a different piece for each place indicated in the script, or wherever you decide to have music. You will record all of these selections onto a "music cassette." Then, on another cassette, the "final cassette," you will mix music with voices: Record the characters' lines as you read through the script, and at a place where music is suggested, record the selection you have made from the music cassette on the final cassette. When you are finished combining words, music, and sound effects on the final cassette, you will have the sound track for your show.

The most time-consuming part of the process is finding the right music. Once you have done this, it will take you from one to two hours to make the sound track. Obviously, it takes longer to make the tape than it will to play it when it is finished. The additional time will be taken up looking over scripts, cueing the music tape, listening to newly taped sections, and rerecording parts you find unsatisfactory.

What you will need to make a sound track

To create a sound track with music, you will need two tape recorders and two blank cassette tapes. Portable cassette recorders work well, especially those with two speakers. If possible, try to use recorders that play without static, humming, or other background noise.

To make the final cassette, it is best to use a recorder with a condenser microphone (a tiny patch labeled "mic"), since it will result in better sound quality. A condenser microphone works better than a hand-held microphone whenever there are many voices, or music and voice being recorded simultaneously.

Buy the highest-quality tapes you can. Since no show in this book is longer than 20 minutes, a 60-minute tape will be adequate for your sound track. You may consider buying a third tape to make a copy of the final recording, in case something happens to it before the actual performance.

Making the music cassette

Finding music

After looking over your script, decide where you want to have music. In these plays, I suggest using music at the very beginning, while welcoming people to the show; between scenes, to bridge the gap in the action and set the mood for the new scene; during chase/action scenes as exciting background music; and at times when the puppets are singing.

Take the time to choose appropriate music.

Happy music works best at the beginning and end of a play.

Fast-paced music, like much Chopin piano music, second movements of symphonies, and some rock music, works well for chase scenes. Keep an ear tuned for any music that sounds exciting, particularly music with staccato notes.

To bridge gaps, you may need scary-sounding music; sad music; triumphant music; or any music that sounds the way you think the characters are feeling at the time.

Almost always, you will find that music without words is most useful for introductions, gaps between scenes, chase/action scenes, and conclusions.

Make a list of the places in the play where you want to add music. At each place, describe what feeling you want the music to express—for instance, surprise, anger, or fright. If you can, narrow down the choices to a type as well as a mood. For example, both a rock song and a piece of

18

chamber music can express a happy mood; consider which you feel would be more appropriate. Once you have made your list as specific as you can, choose several possible selections for each place in the play from the collection of a public library or a large personal library, if one is available to you. Listen to the different selections and decide which piece or song is the best choice. Since most places in a play will call for no more than a minute of music, you will be able to use only a segment of the piece you have selected. Decide which part is the most important.

Recording the music

Once you have found the musical selections you wish to use in the play, record them onto the "music cassette" in the order you will use them in the play. If possible, tape directly from the original record or tape, using a stereo with a link between the phonograph and the tape deck or a dual tape deck. If you do not have access to equipment of this type, just play the record or tape in a quiet room, and record what you need from it onto the music cassette.

Each musical segment on your music cassette should last from 30 seconds to three minutes, depending on how much you think you will use. Tape a little more music than you think you will need, in order to give yourself greater flexibility in the taping of the final cassette. It is also a good idea to leave approximately 15 seconds between selections on the music cassette.

Making the final cassette

Once you have made your music cassette and looked over the script, you will be ready to make the final recording of the performance. It's important to tape in a quiet room free from such interruptions as outside conversation, the barking of a dog, the ringing of a telephone, or the opening of a door. These noises will be picked up on the tape and may spoil the mood of the play.

Of course, one puppeteer can assume more than one role, changing his or her voice, adding inflections, and so forth. But it's best to have several people on hand to read the various parts. Before assigning parts, consider who might sound best in a particular role. Each person should have his or her own script, if possible. Keep the scripts flat and urge everyone to turn the pages carefully, making as little noise as possible.

Group the cast around one tape recorder—preferably one with a condenser microphone—and insert a rewound blank tape. This tape will become the final cassette. Have the music cassette ready in another tape recorder.

Start the final cassette recording, making sure it moves past the white part of the tape at the beginning (anything said during that portion of the tape will not record). Turn on the music cassette to the selection of opening music. After at least 15 seconds, turn down the volume slightly—low enough so that the narrator can be heard above it, but high enough so that the tune can still be heard. After the narrator reads the introductory lines, the music cassette should be turned up for several seconds. Wait until the end of a musical phrase or section to turn off the music completely. When you do, use the "pause" rather than the "stop" button; it will make less noise on the final cassette. At the same time, pause the final cassette and then turn both recorders off.

Rewind the final cassette and listen to it. Is the music loud enough? Can the narrator's voice be heard clearly at the same time?

Once you are satisfied with the opening of the play, continue making the final cassette, adding music where appropriate. Remember to leave time for the actions of the characters as you go along. If a character is looking around a new place, pause briefly between lines to let her take it in, just as she would in real life. If a character needs to shake hands with another, or to cross the stage to sign something or pick something up, leave time for the puppet to do so. You should imagine acting the scene out as you make the sound track, so that you do not leave too much or too little time for actions.

Keep in mind that during a chase/action scene, lively music is not enough to convey an exciting mood. The characters should add lines such as, "Oh, no!" and "Help!" to make the actions seem more real.

As you go along, you will need to add not only music, but sound effects. Almost anything you need for sound effects can be found in an average household. For instance, you can strike a glass or metal bowl with a fork or butter knife to produce a clang. Sometimes the best sound effects are made with your own voice—this is true for most humming, the buzzing of an insect, an animal growling or barking, and the sound of cheering. If you use your imagination and experiment a little bit, you will have no trouble making as many and as varied sound effects as you wish.

Give each character his own voice: his own pitch, accent, and pace. You may wish to enliven the voices of some characters by adding laughs, coughs, hisses, or other speech traits. No matter how strange you make your character's voice, be sure to speak clearly and somewhat more slowly than you would in real life. It is especially important that the audience be able to hear every word the characters say, because the puppets will not move their lips and gesture as real speakers do.

Remember that during a performance several things will have to be done between acts—closing and opening curtains, changing sets, gathering props, and positioning puppeteers for the opening of a new act—so as you tape, leave at least 20 seconds between acts. You may even want to have music and between-act narration (taped over music in the same way as the introduction, or delivered without any music), which can last as long as 40 to 45 seconds.

As you continue through the tape, take the time to rewind and check it frequently, making sure that you have been recording everything you want, that the sound effects are convincing, and that the timing and reading of lines are smooth. Also, when you have finished the tape, listen to the entire recording immediately, timing it and checking it once more for errors.

Finally, remember to have fun making the sound track. It is impossible to create an absolutely perfect tape, and most minor errors will not be noticed by an audience in the finished production.

◆◆ 5 Rehearsal and Performance

O nce you have finished the final cassette, bring all the puppets, sets, and props behind the puppet stage. Place the sets on the backdrop, one on top of the other, with the set for the last act on the bottom, and the set for the first act on top. Most of the plays in this book call for at least one set to be used two to four times during a play, in which case you will have to take a set off the top and put it back on several times during the performance.

Bend the hangers to get the sets to fit on top of one another without falling off the backdrop, and check once again to make sure each set can be viewed clearly from the audience.

Choosing parts

One person can operate more than one puppet, even in the same act, so you can conceivably have twice as many puppets onstage as there are puppeteers. When assigning parts, keep in mind that it is not necessary for the person who spoke one character's lines on the tape to operate that puppet. Instead, consider whether any puppets have particularly big or small heads; these will be operated most easily by the puppeteers with the largest or smallest hands. You might also think about how much each puppet moves onstage. This is especially important in acts where there are several puppets onstage at once, making it necessary for puppeteers to work two at a time. Whenever possible, the person operating a puppet that is onstage for much of an act should either not operate any other puppets in that act or operate another that has a brief appearance only.

Rehearsing the show

Now you can practice your show, act by act. Begin by playing Act I on the final cassette while looking over the stage directions. Discuss the action with the other puppeteers to get a general sense of who has to be where when. Then restart the final cassette and try to perform the first act. Practice the act over and over, making adjustments as needed. You may have to adjust the positioning of puppets onstage, the timing of entrances and exits, and the interaction among the puppets. Practice using the props and gesturing with the puppets to make sure that you can do so effectively and in the time allowed on the sound track.

A puppet should enter and exit the stage from the side, just as a person would walk onto a stage. Be sure not to make puppets appear from below or disappear straight downward, as though there were a trap door under the stage. You should reserve such sudden appearances and disappearances for magical surprises.

Make your puppets act alive! If they are afraid, have them shake or hide their eyes; perhaps they will cower in a corner of the stage. If they are feeling brave, make them step jauntily when they walk. If they are confused, or new to a situation, have them look around, bewildered. A curious character can scurry around and peek out here and there behind other puppets, or from the side windows when not on the mainstage. Puppets can jump up and down, point, gesture with their hands, and much more. Two puppets can hug, pat each other on the head or back, shake hands, fight, dance, pull or drag something, or hand each other things.

The puppet who is speaking at a given moment should move his head and sometimes his body. The other puppets should restrict their movements, so it is clear that they are not the ones speaking. However, even the puppets who are not speaking can make some type of movement. They can look at the speaker, nod "yes" or "no," look scared at the mention of a monster, sneak off, or exchange glances with another puppet. If your characters are lively, they will be more likely to hold the attention of an audience, particularly if it is composed of young children.

Remember to use the side windows effectively. They may be used during interludes between acts or as "second sets" representing another location during an act. Characters can peek out of side windows to watch what is happening on the mainstage. As mentioned earlier, side windows can also be used to increase the excitement of chase/action scenes, which involve intense interaction among the characters. A chase/action scene consists of a chase, struggle, ambush, or other lively physical activity, such as dancing or playing. Such scenes are crucial if you wish to hold the attention of young children in the audience. They also provide some of the greatest excitement and plot development in the play.

A chase scene offers an opportunity to use all three parts of the puppet stage (main stage and two side windows) at once. Puppets may, for example, run across the main stage and exit on one side, reappear in the window on that side, then run back across and appear in the other side window. Or, they may unexpectedly run first one way, and then immediately change direction. They may keep appearing in different places throughout the interlude, which will usually be accompanied by music. Any combination you find exciting is a good one, and you will often improvise a little in each performance. The scene can be very exciting, particularly when two or more puppets are rushing out here and there, one sometimes chasing close behind another across the main stage. The only limiting factor is that the action should be completed when the music and sound effects stop.

One of the puppeteers backstage, or better still, a director, should watch from outside the stage during the rehearsals. He or she can give the puppeteers directions from an audience's point of view. Here are some examples of the types of suggestions a director might make: "Hold Mr. Pleasant's head up more"; "The skunk should not be taller than the tree— pull the skunk a little lower, hold the tree higher"; "I can see the hand of the person working Jody"; "Androcles doesn't look scared enough; make him shake more"; "Why is the Mother Turtle looking off to the left instead of at the baby turtle she is talking to?"; "I can't tell who is speaking here. Katie should move less when John is talking, and he should move his head more."

Practice until you feel confident that you know what will happen next on the sound track and you can perform the puppets' actions smoothly and naturally. During your last rehearsals, be sure to perform the play in its entirety, without interruption, ironing out any problems you may have with props, scene changes, puppet switches, and chase/action scenes.

The performance

Finally, you are ready to perform! You may want to make programs, giving the name of the person who speaks the lines for each character, and who is controlling each puppet. The tape recorder should be placed so that

24

the audience can hear the voices clearly, and the volume can be adjusted easily from backstage, if need be. If you have speakers, place them in the front of the room on either side of the stage. Give the audience time to assemble and to become quiet. If you are performing inside, you may choose to dim the lights and spotlight the stage, but it is not necessary.

Start the sound track, and begin the play!

Even though you will have to concentrate closely on what you are doing, enjoy yourself. If you make a minor or even a major mistake, do not be concerned; just keep performing the play, fixing the situation as best you can. Concentrate on making your puppets come to life. You have worked hard to create this puppet show, and you should feel proud of it.

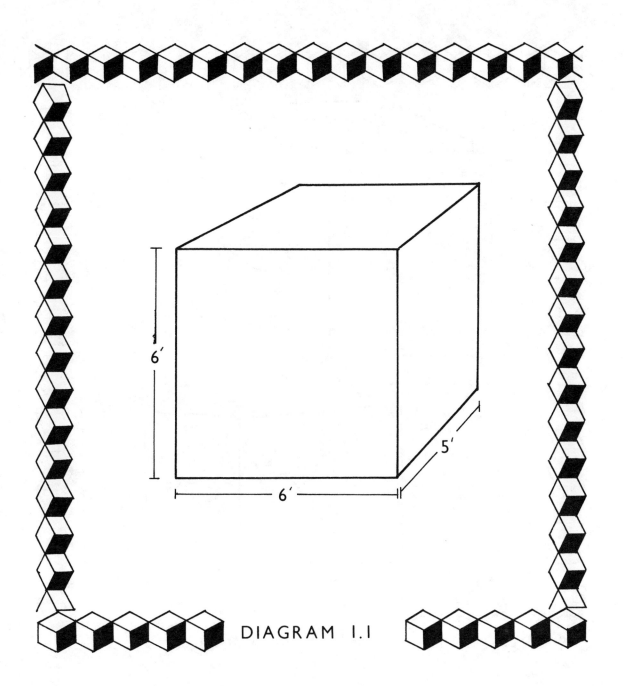

DIAGRAM 1.1

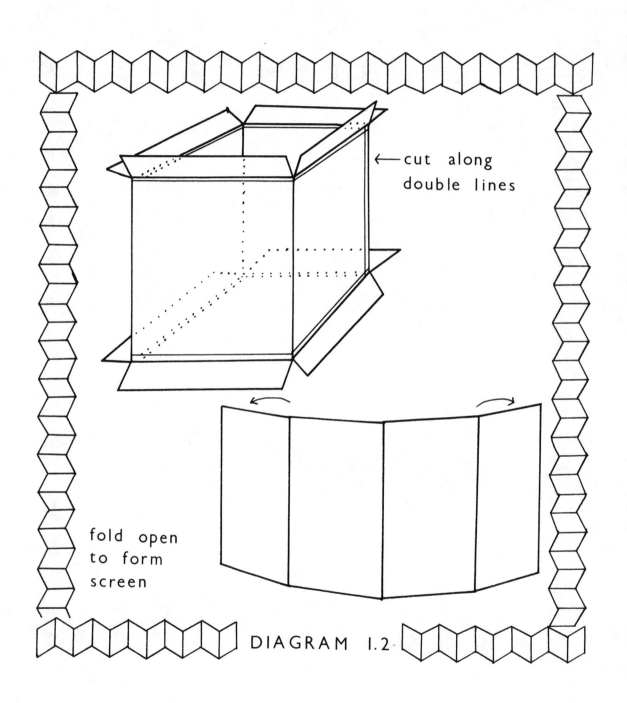

← cut along double lines

fold open
to form
screen

DIAGRAM 1.2

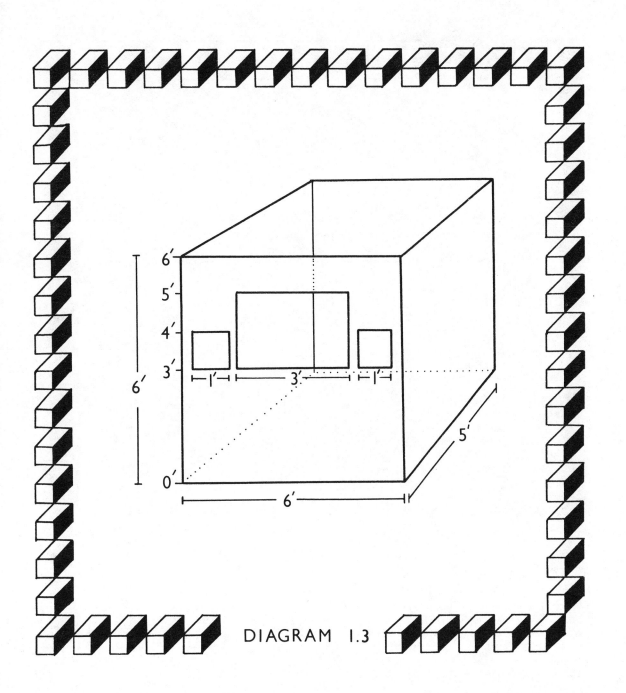

DIAGRAM 1.3

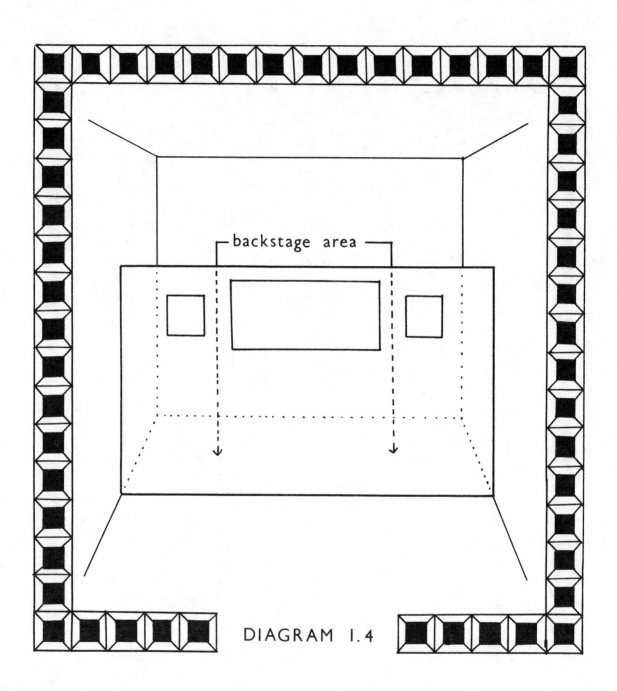

backstage area

DIAGRAM 1.4

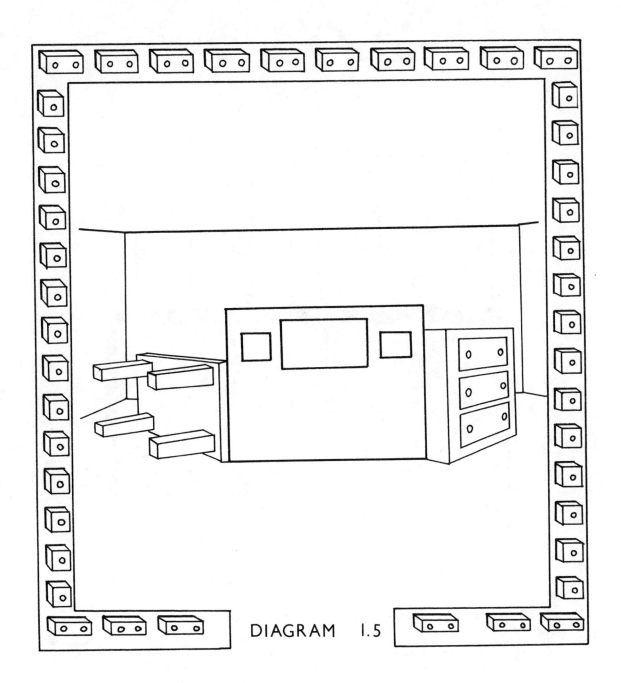

DIAGRAM 1.5

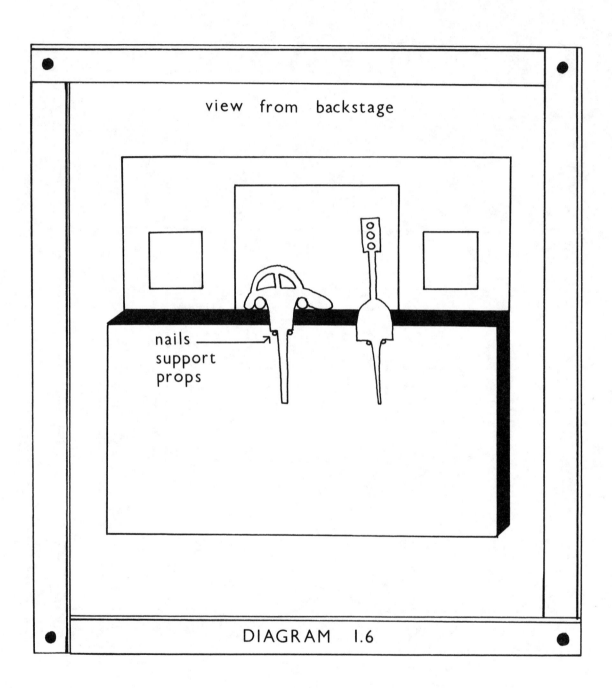

view from backstage

nails
support
props

DIAGRAM 1.6

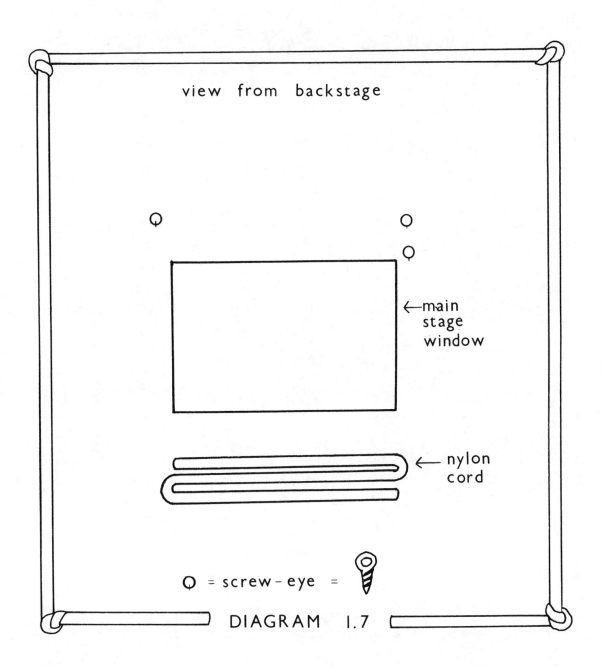

view from backstage

←main
stage
window

←nylon
cord

○ = screw-eye =

DIAGRAM 1.7

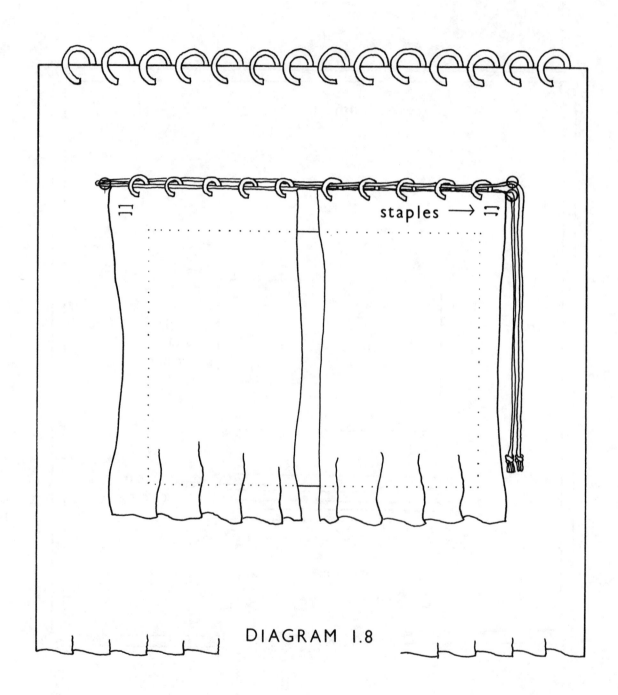

staples →

DIAGRAM 1.8

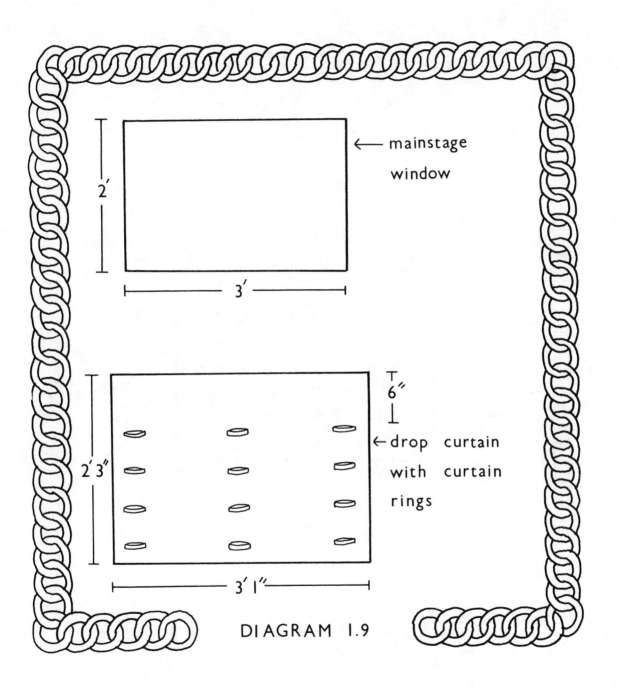

DIAGRAM 1.9

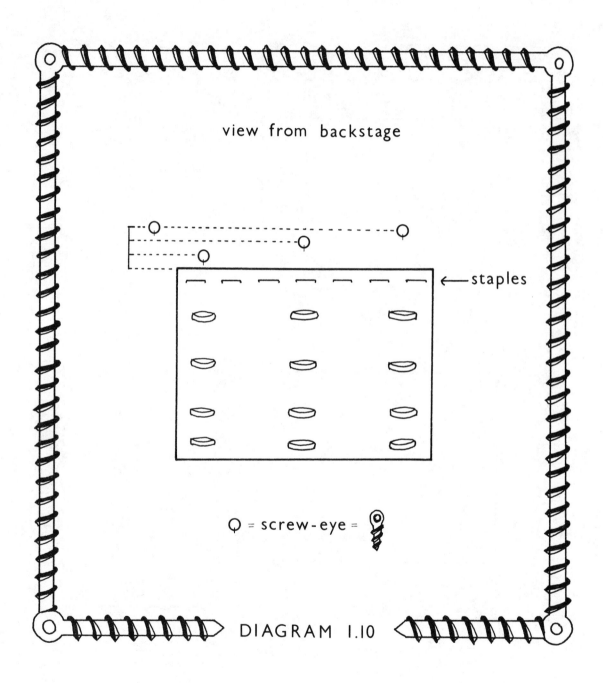

view from backstage

staples

Q = screw-eye = 🔩

DIAGRAM 1.10

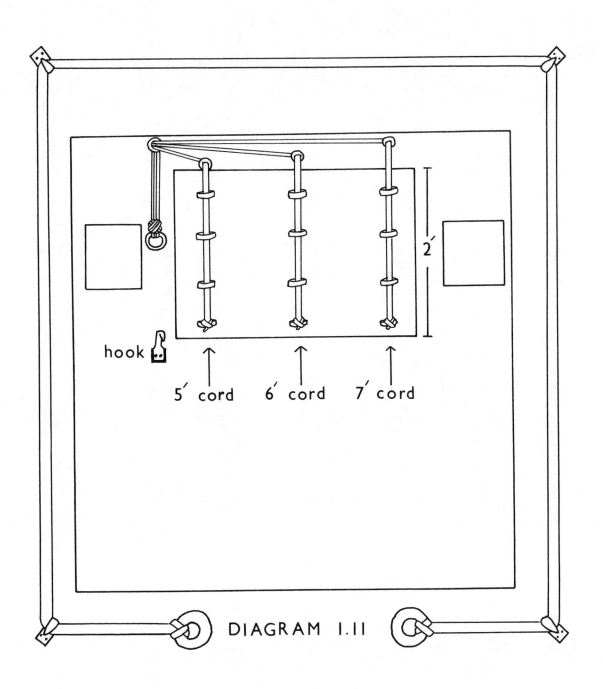

hook

2′

5′ cord   6′ cord   7′ cord

DIAGRAM 1.11

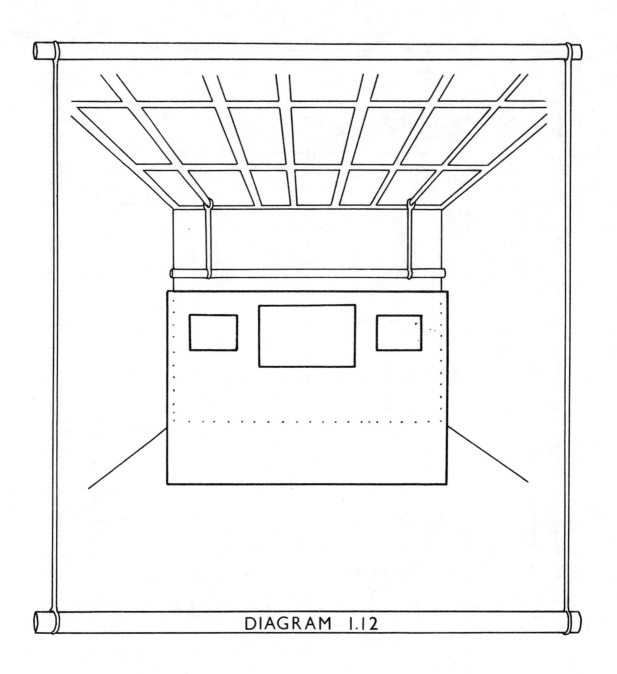

DIAGRAM 1.12

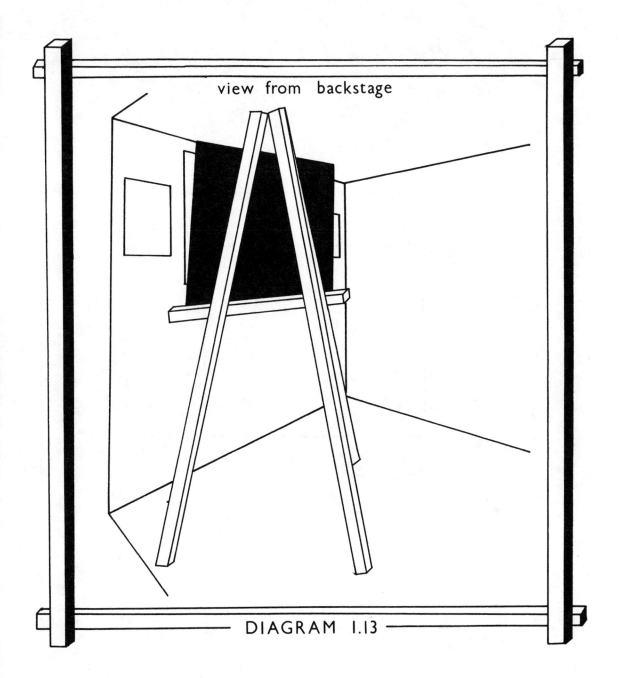

view from backstage

DIAGRAM 1.13

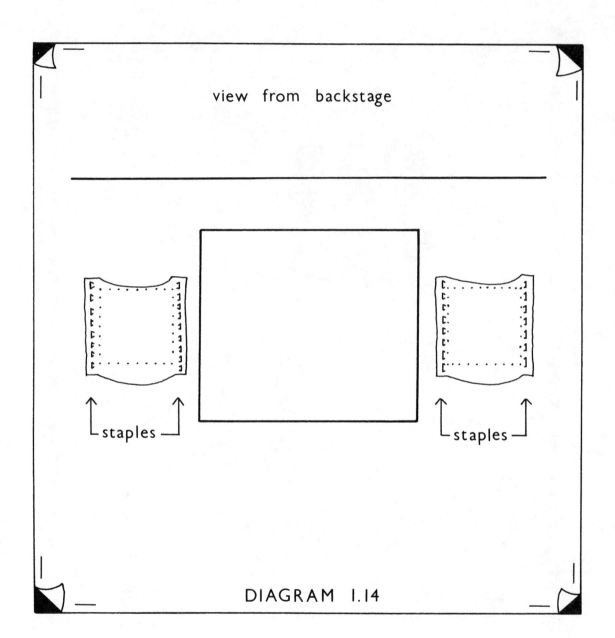

view from backstage

staples

staples

DIAGRAM 1.14

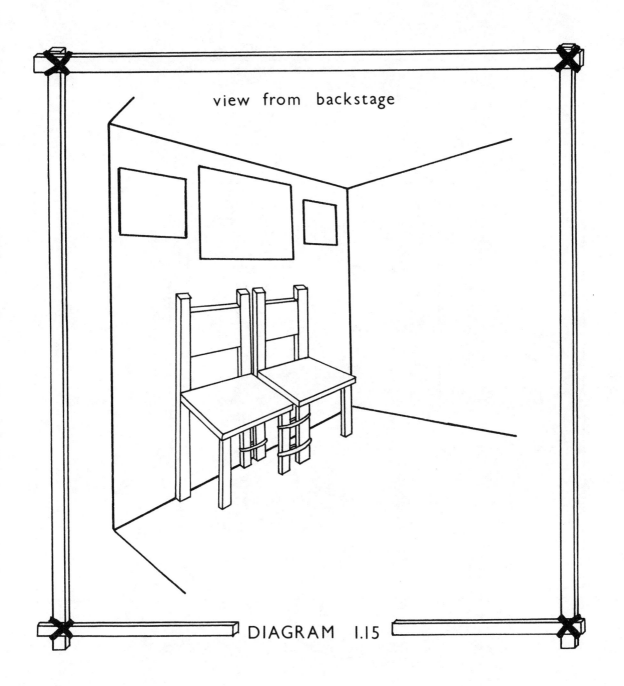

view from backstage

DIAGRAM 1.15

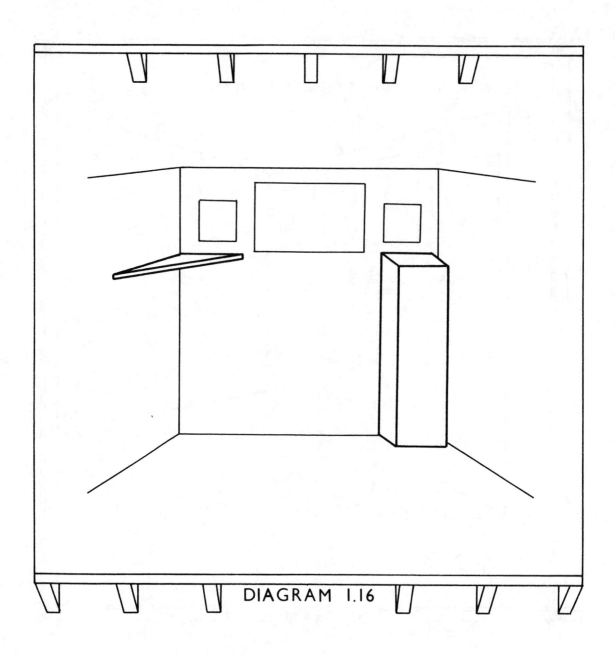

DIAGRAM 1.16

DIAGRAM 1.17

DIAGRAM 1.18

use blanket
stitch for
armholes

DIAGRAM 1.19

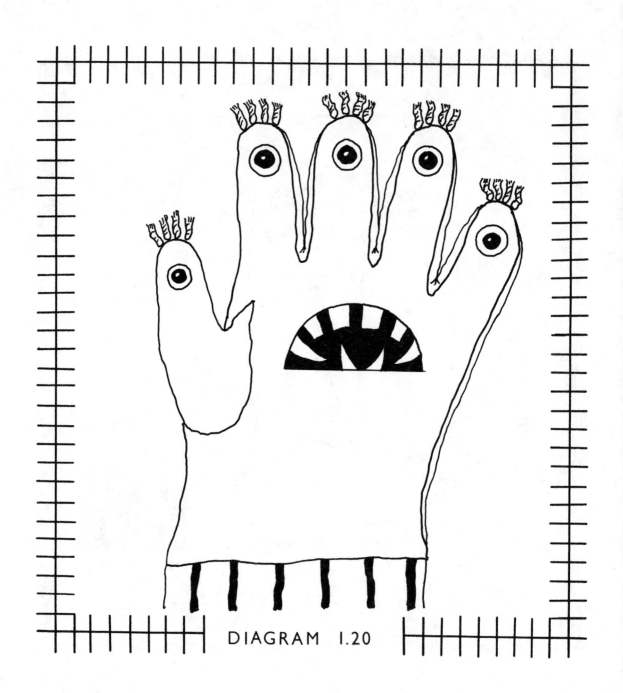

DIAGRAM 1.20

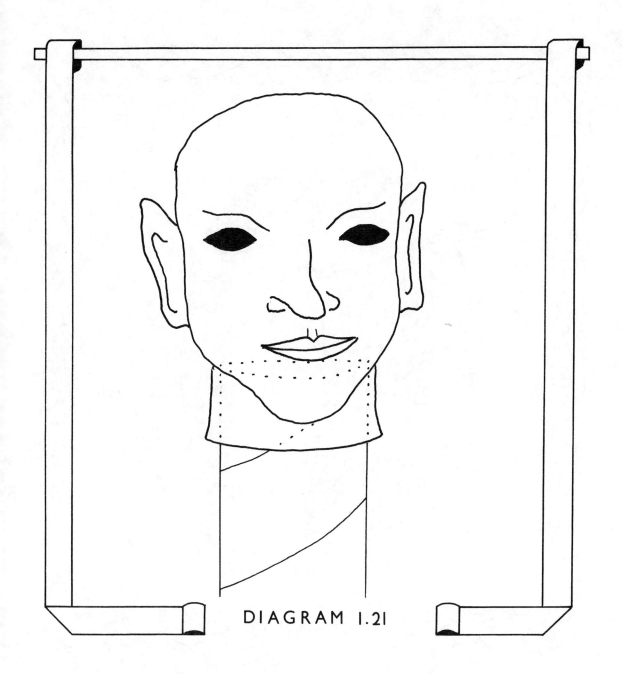

DIAGRAM 1.21

DIAGRAM 1.22

DIAGRAM 1.23

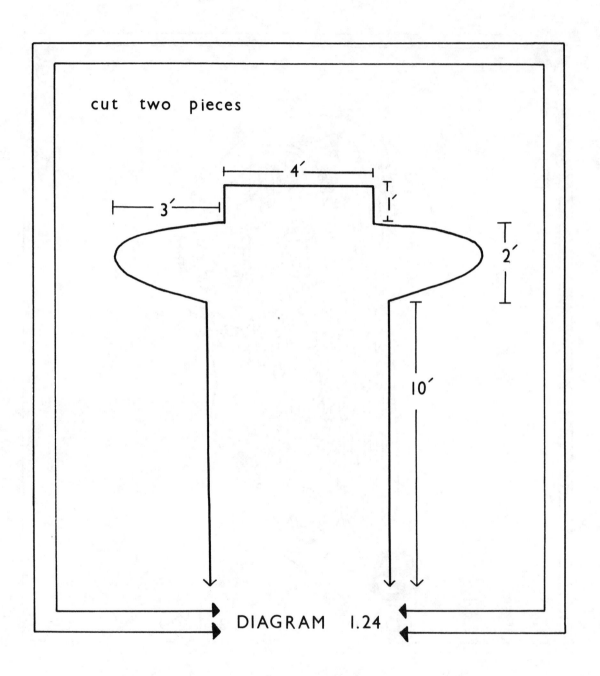

cut   two   pieces

4′

3′

1′

2′

10′

DIAGRAM   1.24

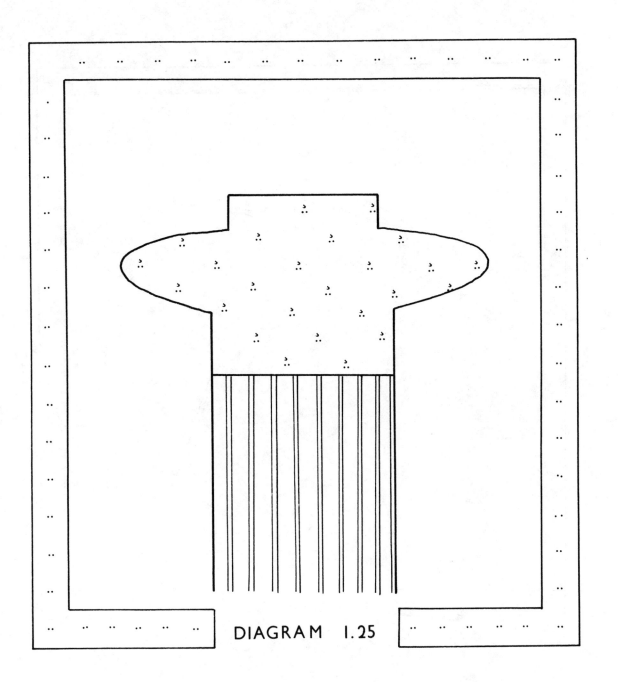

DIAGRAM 1.25

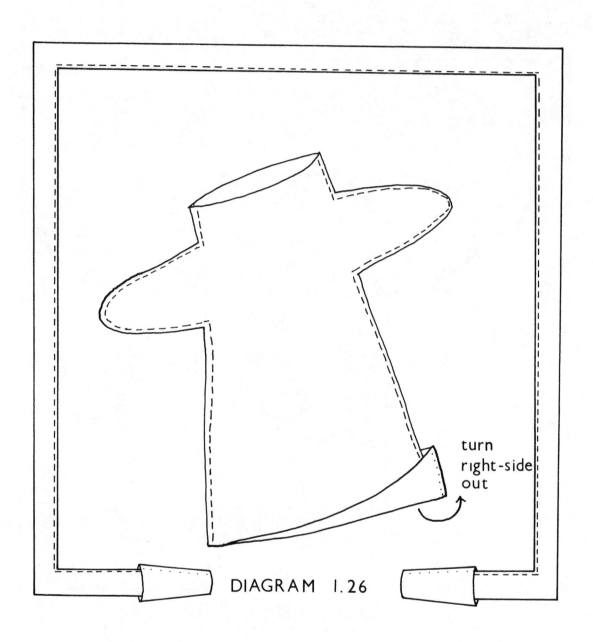

turn
right-side
out

DIAGRAM 1.26

DIAGRAM 1.27

DIAGRAM 1.28

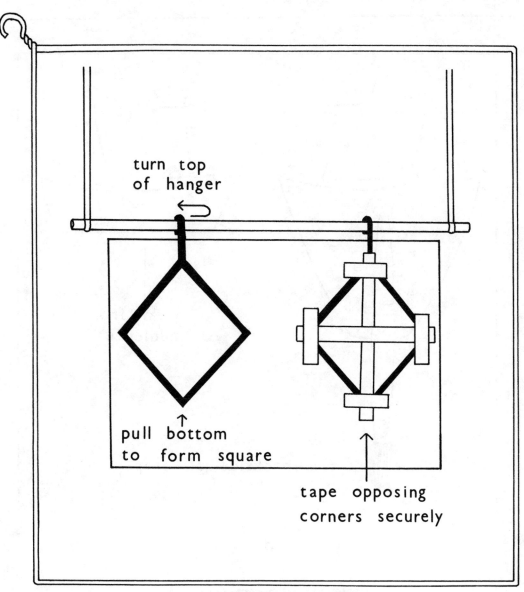

turn top
of hanger

pull bottom
to form square

tape opposing
corners securely

DIAGRAM 1.29

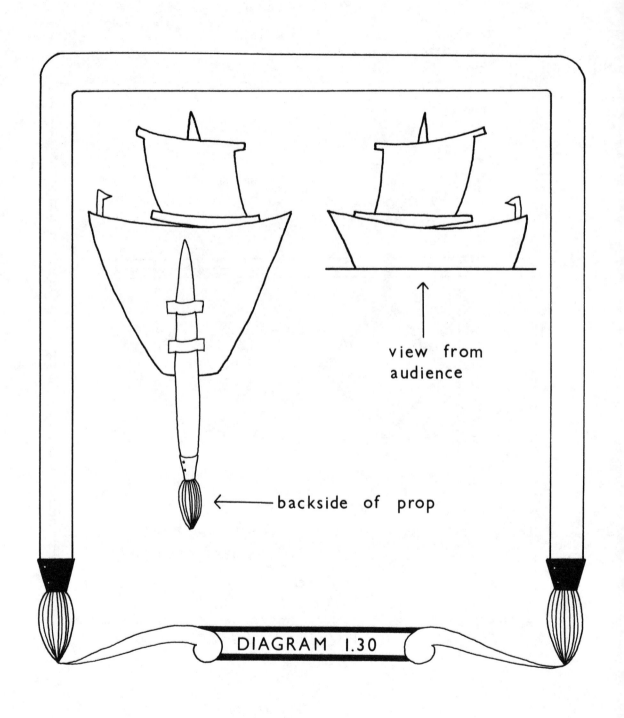

view from
audience

← backside of prop

DIAGRAM 1.30

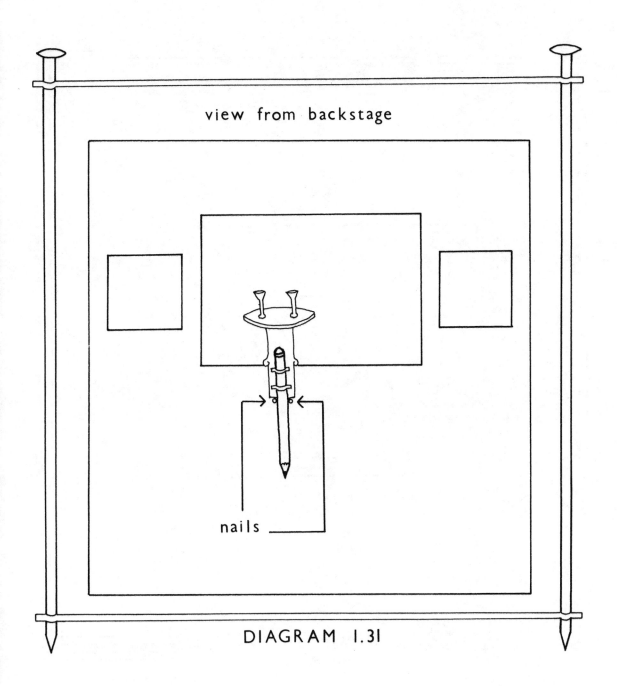

view from backstage

nails

DIAGRAM 1.31

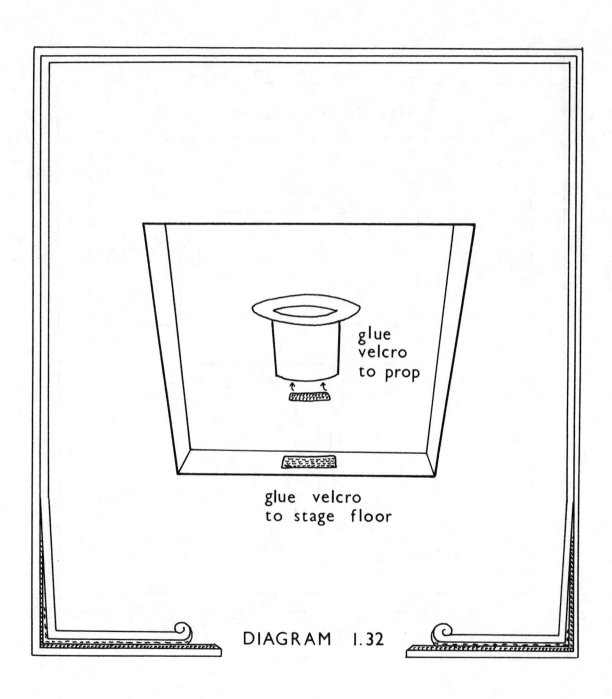

glue
velcro
to prop

glue velcro
to stage floor

DIAGRAM 1.32

attach velcro
to front of
arm and
back of prop

additional
velcro may
be attached
elsewhere

DIAGRAM 1.33

PART II
The Plays

The Story of Possum

◆◆◆ The Story of Possum

Adapted from the bedtime story
by Henry Buchwald

Cast:
POSSUM, *first a caterpillar, then a butterfly*
WISE OLD OWL
NARRATOR

Sets:
Meadow
Woodland lake

Props:
Cocoon

ACT I

Happy, introductory music is played for several seconds, and then turned down.

NARRATOR: Hello. Welcome to our puppet show. *The Story of Possum* is adapted from the family bedtime story by Henry Buchwald. Every time Possum says, "Oh, come now, Mr. Owl," we invite you to join him in saying, "I'll never be a butterfly." You may get used to saying this, but be prepared for a surprise at the end. (*The music is turned up briefly, and then off. Curtain opens on the meadow.* POSSUM *wriggles back and forth along the stage, eating and looking about.*) Once upon a time, there was a young caterpillar with the unusual name of Possum. He had an unusual friend, too—an owl.

One day, Possum was wriggling through the grass, which was as tall as great trees to him. He was working very hard to find tender leaves to eat, so that he would grow and become longer and fatter. His friend Wise Old Owl saw him, and he swooped down from the sky to join him. (WISE OLD OWL *swoops onto stage from above, then lands near* POSSUM.)

OWL: Good morning, Possum!

POSSUM: Good morning, Mr. Owl. How are you today?

OWL: Fine, thank you. I see that you are becoming long and fat. Soon you will be very tired. You will spin yourself a house, called a cocoon, and you will have a long, long sleep. When you wake up, you will no longer be a caterpillar, but a beautiful butterfly.

POSSUM: Oh, come now, Mr. Owl. I'll never be a butterfly. I have been a caterpillar all my life, and all my friends are caterpillars, too! (POSSUM *and* OWL *move about on stage for a few seconds, each looking for food.*)

NARRATOR: For days and days, Possum ate and ate. Owl greeted him less cheerily, because whenever he told Possum about spinning his cocoon and taking a long sleep and changing into a butterfly, Possum would just smile and answer—(*As* POSSUM *speaks the following lines,* OWL *covers his eyes and shakes his head in exasperation.*)

POSSUM: Oh, come now, Mr. Owl. I'll never be a butterfly. I have been a caterpillar all my life, and all my friends are caterpillars, too. (OWL *hops angrily offstage. There is a short pause before* NARRATOR *speaks. During pause and narration,* POSSUM *pretends to be drawing a thread from the side of the stage. A corner of the cocoon appears and* POSSUM *keeps pretending to weave it and pull it. More and more of the cocoon appears onstage, and* POSSUM *disappears into it, until only his head sticks out.*)

NARRATOR (*Very slowly*): One day, Possum felt very fat and very tired. He wanted to take a long nap and didn't wish to be disturbed, so he spun a house with himself inside. Just as he sealed the last crack in his house, he heard the familiar voice of his friend, the Owl. (OWL *flies onstage and lands near cocoon.*)

OWL: When you wake up, you will be a beautiful butterfly! (POSSUM *pulls his head into cocoon. During next part of narration,* OWL *leans this way and that, looking at cocoon. He taps it and puts his ear up to it.)*

NARRATOR: Possum slept and slept. Each morning, as he returned from a night of hunting, Owl would look at Possum's cocoon to see if Possum was ready to come out.

One day, Owl saw the cocoon moving. (*During next part of narration, cocoon rocks a little, and* POSSUM *slowly emerges with his wings on.* OWL *jumps back, stares, and beats his wings in excitement.*) Suddenly a small opening appeared. The opening became larger and larger and slowly, very unsure of himself, there emerged a beautiful butterfly, with wings of many colors. The butterfly opened his eyes and saw the Owl.

POSSUM (*Sleepily*): Good morning, Owl. I must have slept and slept. (OWL *jumps up and down and flaps his wings.*)

OWL (*Triumphantly*): See, Possum, I told you so! I told you so! I told you that you would be very tired, spin a cocoon, sleep and sleep, and come out as a butterfly.

POSSUM (*Patiently*): Oh, come now, Mr. Owl. I'll never be a butterfly. I have been a caterpillar all my life and all my friends are caterpillars, too. (*During the following narration,* POSSUM *jerkily tries to move along ground. He looks at his wings on either side, and then, slowly, and to his surprise, begins to fly.* OWL *hops to the center of the stage, and* POSSUM *flies back and forth above his head.*)

NARRATOR: But when Possum tried to crawl, he found that he was no longer able to move his body in great waves. Instead, he felt something strange on his sides—they were wings!—and instead of creeping on the tree branch, he found himself up in the air. He was flying!

Possum could not believe that he was really flying, could not believe that he was really a butterfly. All this time, Owl was jumping up and down, shouting:

OWL: You're flying! You're a butterfly! Possum, you're not a caterpillar any more!

POSSUM: Oh, come now, Mr. Owl. I am not a butterfly. I have been a caterpillar all my life, and all my friends are caterpillars, too.

OWL: Fly into the woods and look for the big lake, Possum. Look into the lake and you will see yourself! (POSSUM *flies offstage.* OWL *hops after him a few steps, then flies offstage. Curtain closes. Music plays for a few seconds, then is turned down during the beginning of the following narration.)*

* * * * *

ACT II

NARRATOR: Possum slowly and unsteadily flew toward the woods. By the time he reached the lake, he was no longer having any problem flying. Indeed, he was enjoying it. *(Curtain opens on woodland lake set. The music is turned off. POSSUM flies onto the stage. He hovers and looks around throughout the following scene.)*

When Possum flew over the clear and still water of the woodland lake, he saw himself reflected in the water. So, he thought, it's true. He was not a caterpillar any more, but a beautiful butterfly with wings shining in the sunlight!

Then Possum noticed that there were many other butterflies looking at their reflections in the lake. *(OWL may appear in a side window, or peek around main stage from behind.)* And Possum cried out happily:

POSSUM: Now I *am* a butterfly—and all my friends are butterflies, too! *(OWL smiles, nods, waves to audience. POSSUM flies offstage, and OWL disappears from side window. The curtain closes. Happy music is heard.)*

ALL: *The End!*

Production Notes
THE STORY OF POSSUM

Puppets

Possum

Possum is a sock puppet with a reinforced movable mouth, eyes, and antennae. You may decorate him with fabric pens, if you wish.

Possum's wings may be made by using wire, glue, and delicate, shimmery fabric in a pastel color. Form 24-19 gauge wire into the shape of a set of wings with a "spine" down the middle. Twine the wire ends securely, to hold the shape of the wings.

Double the fabric and hold it against the wire frame, leaving an extra quarter inch of material all around, then cut the fabric into the shape of the wings. (You will have cut two

66

pieces of fabric.) Put glue all along the wire. Place one cut piece of cloth on top of the wire and press it into the glue. Hold the fabric in place for several minutes, until the glue dries. Turn the frame over and glue the second piece of material to the other side. The edges need not be joined, as long as the wire frame is hidden. Carefully bend the wings into shape.

Possum's wings will need to be attached very quickly. The puppeteer will make him disappear inside the cocoon, put the wings onto him, and lift him back into the cocoon so that he can emerge as a butterfly. Snaps or Velcro that blend in with the color of the wings' fabric may be used to attach the wings to the body. Sew two or three pieces of Velcro or snaps onto the back of Possum's body, and attach corresponding pieces of Velcro or snaps, spaced the same distance apart, to the bottom of the pair of wings, along the spine.

Wise Old Owl

The owl puppet may have a cloth body and papier-mâché head with a beak, big eyes, and small pointed ears, or be made completely out of cloth. This puppet should be fairly short, neither towering over Possum the caterpillar nor getting in the way of Possum when he is a flying butterfly. To make the owl's body rounded, sew stuffing into the cloth of the body, or wrap fabric around the puppeteer's hand and arm before he puts on the puppet. (This latter method does, however, make it impossible to change puppeteers in the middle of the show. The puppeteer must also take care not to let the stuffing fall out during the performance.)

Sets

Meadow

This set can be painted with grass and various-sized flowers, all of which should be much taller than Possum.

Woodland lake

Paint a lake with several brightly colored butterflies hovering over it. The lake and the butterflies are by far the most important parts of the set, but you may add lily pads or rocks that rise out of the water. The lake may also have pebbles, grass, or flowers on its banks.

Props

Cocoon

A beautiful cocoon can be made of shimmery, lightweight white fabric attached to a frame of thick wire in the shape of a half-sphere—similar to an umbrella. To make the frame, cut four pieces of 18 gauge wire, each two feet long, and one piece four feet long. Bend the long piece into a full circle, twining the ends together to keep the shape. Now bend the four shorter pieces into semi-circles. Wrap the ends of each semi-circle to the large circle, forming arched spokes. Connect the centers of the four arches with another piece of wire or strong tape.

Next, cut a piece of fabric larger than the frame. Put glue on the frame and press the cloth down on top of it. You may leave some fabric hanging down, or you may glue the extra fabric to the inside of the frame. A long heavy twist of wire or other material may serve as a handle for the cocoon.

Instead of wire, you may use a tall hat or similarly shaped object as a frame, or make one out of papier-mâché. Such a frame will be sturdier and easier to cover with fabric, and may even be painted; however, it will look heavier and less like a spun object, and won't have the light, shimmery effect of the wire cocoon.

Notes on performance

• *The Story of Possum* is the simplest play to perform in this book, and for this reason, the simplest possible stage—one without side windows—may be used. If you do have one or more side windows, there is a suggestion for their use at the end of the play. If not, Owl will simply peek around onto the main stage from offstage, or not appear at all at the end of the play.

• While Possum is still a caterpillar, he should inch and wiggle across the stage. Most of the puppeteer's forearm may be placed flat on the stage, as long as the puppet is long enough and the rest of the puppeteer's body remains hidden.

• Possum's wings should be attached while Possum is "in the cocoon." He should then emerge from the cocoon slowly, his wings and full body coming into view just as the narrator says, "butterfly."

• Possum can appear to fly by moving up and down in the air and tilting slightly from side to side, so that the wings move from side to side, as though flapping.

To create the effect of Possum flying around Owl's head (end of Act I), Owl should be lowered a little behind the stage. The puppet should also tilt its head back and to the side, looking up at Possum. The puppeteer operating Possum should be sure to cross over behind the puppeteer operating Owl, so that Possum flies all around the stage, not just in one area.

Funky and the Animals

◆◆ Funky and the Animals

A rock musical

Cast:
    FUNKY, *a kangaroo*
    SMART ALEX, *a mouse*
    OMAR, *a bear*
    BRIGHTY, *a dog*
    RAY, *pet shop owner*
    SLIMY, *a snake*
    OFFSTAGE VOICES
    DIRECTOR
    NARRATOR

Sets:
    Ray's Pet Shop
    City street
    Auditorium

Props:
    Cage in Ray's Pet Shop
    Runaway sacks (optional)
    Two guitars
    Microphone
    Drum set
    Truck
    Net

ACT I

NARRATOR: Hello! Welcome to our play, *Funky and the Animals*. This story begins in the pet shop of a man named Ray. One day, while Ray is out, some of the animals try to entertain themselves by singing. . . . *(Curtain opens to reveal* FUNKY, SMART ALEX, OMAR, *and* BRIGHTY *in a big cage in Ray's Pet Shop. Rock music can be heard. Animals are singing and dancing around.)*

RAY *(Appearing in side window):* Stop making all that racket! *(Hands over ears)* Stop! Stop, you little monsters! I SAID STOP!!! *(As* RAY *comes on stage, singing stops.)* What are you trying to do—destroy my business? Nobody is going to want to buy loud screeching pets! No dinner for you tonight, and . . . and if I catch you singing or making trouble again, you'll be sorry.

SMART ALEX *(Mimicking* RAY): You'll be sorry . . . nah-nah-nah-nah-nah!

RAY *(Sharply):* I heard that, Smart Alex; and just for that, you're going to be Slimy the Snake's lunch tomorrow. *(*RAY *laughs as he exits.* SLIMY *appears in one of side windows, sticking his head out and around to look at* SMART ALEX *as he speaks.)*

SLIMY *(With a sinister, hissing laugh):* I'll be sssseeing you sssssoon!! *(*SLIMY *draws his head back somewhat, but remains visible in window. As* SLIMY *repeatedly opens his mouth wide and closes it, he can be heard snoring.* FUNKY, OMAR, *and* BRIGHTY *settle down quietly, as though they are sleeping.)*

NARRATOR: Later that evening, all the pets are asleep, except for Smart Alex, who is miserable at the thought of becoming Slimy's main course the next day.

SMART ALEX *(Upset):* Oh, why did I have to open my big mouth! It gets me into so much trouble all the time. *(Sighs unhappily. He then sings a sad song, like "Yesterday," by the Beatles. After a short time, the other pets wake up.)*

BRIGHTY: Sh-h! Smart Alex, you shouldn't be singing. That slinky spy Slimy is sure to tell Ray on you.

SMART ALEX: But I'm already in the worst trouble possible! I have to get out of here. There must be some way to escape.

FUNKY: We could all use a break from this place. Let's split.

OMAR: Even if there were a life out there for us, how could we ever escape from here? And what would we do if we got out? Nobody wants us, and we have no place to go.

SMART ALEX (*Hopefully*): I'll bet Brighty could think of a good plan.

BRIGHTY: Well, I do have an idea. . . . (*Animals huddle together and mumble.*) So, have you got this now? Smart Alex is going to tease Slimy. Then Slimy will be so angry, he will open the door to snatch Alex. When he does, we'll all make a run for it.

FUNKY: Wow, man! Just like one big stampede! (*SLIMY's snoring is heard again, now more loudly than before. Animals whisper together.*)

SMART ALEX (*Taunting*): Nah, nah . . . you slimy old snake, you're not going to have *me* for lunch. You're nothing but a big slinky!

SLIMY (*Sputtering as he wakes up*): Hissss! Watch your ssstep, you mangy moussse. I might not wait until tomorrow. Sssss.

SMART ALEX: You chicken! (*Imitating a chicken*) Bok-bok-bok! Poor baby snake, you can't do anything without Ray! You're all hiss and no action. If you were really brave, you'd try to catch me and eat me now.

SLIMY: Ssss! All right, big mouth. That'sss a challenge I cannot refusssse! (*SLIMY slithers onto main stage. He opens cage door to get at SMART ALEX. Animals run out, stepping on him as they go. Chase music plays while SLIMY chases them around, hissing all the while. Animals escape. The curtain closes.*)

* * * * *

ACT II

NARRATOR: After Funky, Smart Alex, Omar, and Brighty manage to escape, they find themselves free—and unemployed—in the big city. (*Curtain opens on city set with storefronts, restaurants, and a theater. FUNKY, OMAR, SMART ALEX, and BRIGHTY enter. Each carries runaway sack over shoulder.*)

FUNKY: Wow, guys. This is it! The big city.

OMAR: It sure is big out here. And I'm hungry.

SMART ALEX: Do you think we can find jobs, Brighty? We'll need money.

BRIGHTY (*Looking at store front windows*): Well, let's look around. Here's a sign: "Superman look-alikes, apply within." No, that's not for us. Hm-m-m. "Movie hall usher—no furry animals need apply." Oh, well. Hey, look over there! "Restaurant help wanted." Let's go apply. (*Animals exit.*)

OFFSTAGE VOICE (*Thundering*): No animals allowed! (*Animals tumble back onstage, as if thrown.*)

SMART ALEX: Ouch! I don't think I want a job after all!

BRIGHTY: Remember, Smart Alex, soon our food will run out, and we still need a place to live.

OMAR: If at first you don't succeed, try, try again.

BRIGHTY: Right. Let's try here. This pretty store window has a sign: "Neiman Marcus seeks elegant, experienced sales attendants with exceptional knowledge of high fashion. Interviews may be arranged within."

FUNKY: Hey, that's trendy, Cats. Let's go! (*Animals exit.*)

OFFSTAGE VOICE (*In high tone*): Sorry. We don't take animals! (*Animals tumble back onstage. They get up slowly, looking sad.*)

SMART ALEX: Nobody wants us. I'm going to have to spend my whole life eating out of garbage cans, just like my Uncle Ned.

OMAR: I'll have to go to Yellowstone Park and raid campers.

FUNKY: Yeah. It's "down under" for me. Way down.

BRIGHTY: Don't give up hope! I don't want to spend my life begging for dog biscuits, either. I want to be my own dog. There must be more openings. (*Looks around*) Wait! Look at that sign! "Auditions. We're looking for a great band. You supply the talent; we supply the instruments and auditorium. Tryouts inside."

FUNKY: That is *so* us! We really *love* to sing. Let's go! (*Animals exit. Curtain*)

* * * * *

ACT III

The curtain opens on the auditorium set. SMART ALEX's *drum set is onstage.* FUNKY *holds a microphone.* BRIGHTY *and* OMAR *have guitars slung around their necks.*

DIRECTOR (*Offstage; impatiently*): O.K. Next. Next. Come on, next act, please! Uh, yes, you there. What's your group's name?

BRIGHTY: Our name is (*Pause—then confidently*) Funky and the Animals.

DIRECTOR: Cute, cute. Has a certain ring to it. O.K. Go ahead.

SMART ALEX *(Trembling):* I'm sc-scared. I can't do it.

OMAR: Don't be scared, Smart Alex. You're a great drummer. I'll be standing right next to you. Ready on the guitar, Brighty?

BRIGHTY: Ready.

FUNKY: One, two—a-one, two, three, four. . . . *(Rock song sung by female vocalist is heard as* SMART ALEX, OMAR, *and* BRIGHTY *play their instruments and* FUNKY *sings. They dance and jump around as they perform for two or three minutes.)*

DIRECTOR: Fantastic! I like your sound, people. I think we can use you.

ANIMALS *(Jumping up and down, patting each other on the back and hugging):* Yeah! Wow! All right! Woo!

DIRECTOR: O.K. Now, go home and practice. You can take these instruments with you. Your opening concert will be tomorrow night. You should have about twenty songs ready. And don't be late, folks, or the show—and your band—will have to be permanently canceled. No time for monkey business in show business. The music industry rolls on with or without you. See you tomorrow. *(Curtain)*

*   *   *   *   *

ACT IV

Curtain opens on city street.

OMAR: Can you believe it? I'm *so* happy!

BRIGHTY: This is wonderful!

SMART ALEX: What a break!

FUNKY: Cosmic!

BRIGHTY: Come on, you guys! I'll use this advance money to get a hotel room for us. If everything goes well, we can start looking for our own apartment soon.

FUNKY: Do you mind if I wait for you right here? I'm beat.

BRIGHTY: That's fine, Funky.

SMART ALEX: Omar and I will go get something for us all to eat. See you soon, Funky. *(All exit except* FUNKY, *who remains on one side of the stage.* RAY *appears in side window on other side of stage.)*

RAY: When I saw the advertisement for the new rock band, I knew it had to be those pesky mongrels. At least I'll have that kangaroo back soon. I will remind them one by one that they cannot be independent. They're all mine—until *I* dispose of them. *(*RAY *appears on stage in truck, holding net and leaning out window. Leaving truck on that side of stage,* RAY *tiptoes toward* FUNKY, *with net raised.* FUNKY *is looking off to the other side and humming or singing to herself, so she does not see him.* RAY *lunges at her with the net.* FUNKY *jumps out of the way just in time.)*

FUNKY *(As she jumps):* Help! *(*RAY *chases* FUNKY *while chase music plays.)*

RAY: I'll get you, Funky!

FUNKY: Help! Someone help me, please! *(Eventually,* RAY *catches* FUNKY *in the net and takes her into truck.* FUNKY *screams as they drive away.)* Help! Hey, cats, come quick! I've been totally bagged. Help! *(*BRIGHTY *enters, followed by* SMART ALEX *and* OMAR, *just as truck is almost out of sight.)*

BRIGHTY: Stop! Stop!

SMART ALEX: Ray kidnapped Funky! What will we do?

OMAR: We have to rescue her.

BRIGHTY: O.K. Here's the plan: Smart Alex, you sneak into the shop when Slimy is sleeping. You'll have to be quiet so you don't wake him up. Tie Slimy's two ends to the posts by the doorway. Omar, you take Ray's giant net out of the storage room. Then I'll get Ray to run into the store. He'll trip over Slimy, and you will catch him in the net. After that, we can get Funky out of there! *(In a lower voice)* I hope. *(Curtain)*

* * * * *

ACT V

The curtain opens on the pet store.

SLIMY *(Snoring):* Ha-Ssss . . . Ha-Sssss! *(*SMART ALEX *sneaks in, and "ties up"* SLIMY *by spreading him across main stage.* SLIMY *wakes up.)* Ssss! Landsss sssakesss! What are you doing to me!

SMART ALEX: O.K. Ready! *(*OMAR *appears with net.* BRIGHTY *appears.* SMART ALEX *exits.)*

BRIGHTY *(Calling):* Hey, Ray! We've come back. But you'd better get here fast if you want to hear our conditions for staying. The first one is: We get all the food we want—catered—every day. *(*RAY *appears in side window.)*

RAY *(To animals):* Conditions! Conditions! Forget it! *(To the audience)* I'll

76

teach them to make conditions. Besides, I know it's a trick. They're just here to free that crazy kangaroo. I hate animals. They're all no-good rascals! *(RAY comes running in. He trips over SLIMY, and OMAR catches him in the net. SMART ALEX and FUNKY come running onstage.)*

FUNKY: Yay! I'm free. Let's beat it!

BRIGHTY: Open all the cages as you go. *(FUNKY, SMART ALEX, OMAR, and BRIGHTY exit, cheering. SLIMY and RAY, who is still in the net, remain onstage.)*

RAY *(Calling off):* You think you're so great, but you are all nothing! You'll be complete flops. Soon you'll be crawling back to me—and you know what? I won't even take you back! *(Curtain closes, with RAY and SLIMY on the outside. As NARRATOR begins to speak, an upbeat rock song can be heard in the background. The animals appear, two in each side window. They bob their heads to the beat and wave at audience.)*

NARRATOR: The animals escaped back to the city. They had frustrated Ray and Slimy so much that the terrible pair never came after them again. That night, Funky and the Animals performed their first of many successful concerts. To this day, they are doing what they do best—singing together, free and happy.

ALL *(After several seconds):* The End!

Production Notes
FUNKY AND THE ANIMALS

Puppets

Slimy

Because Slimy does not have arms, a sock or long oven mitt makes an ideal puppet. Reinforce the mouth with posterboard, if you wish. You may also want to attach a tongue made out of felt. Eyes can be made from buttons, construction paper, or cloth, or purchased at a craft store. You may decorate Slimy's back with strips of felt.

The other animals

Puppets for Funky, Smart Alex, Omar, and Brighty may be purchased or made with papier-mâché heads and cloth bodies, or made completely out of cloth. If you make the puppets, it is a good idea to use furry fabric. Be sure to add tails, whiskers, and ears where necessary.

You may wish to give the animals' costumes little touches that help reveal their character—glasses, hats, bow ties, etc. For instance, Funky could wear a jean jacket, a medallion with the peace sign on it, or dark glasses cut from black construction paper.

Ray

Ray should be made with a papier-mâché head and cloth body.

Sets

Ray's Pet Shop

Ray's Pet Shop can be as simple or elaborate as you wish. Begin by drawing a sign at the top of the set reading, RAY'S PET SHOP. Draw a few cages with or without animals in them, and perhaps an aquarium with fish in it.

You might want to add a counter with a cash register, bird cages hanging from the ceiling, signs giving prices or instructions, pet food, leashes, and other pet supplies. Have fun with the details of the set.

City street

The street set shows store fronts of various types. If you wish, make a theater advertising, in lights, all or part of the following: AUDITIONS. WE'RE LOOKING FOR A GREAT BAND. YOU SUPPLY THE TALENT; WE SUPPLY THE INSTRUMENTS AND AUDITORIUM. TRYOUTS INSIDE.

Auditorium

The auditorium set can be very simple; only the stage needs to be depicted. Use paint, glitter, or shiny wrapping paper to cover the surface of the stage, and add spotlights or footlights (these may be cut out of construction paper and decorated around the rims with glitter).

Props

The cage

You need only to make the front of a cage to give the impression that the animals are enclosed. You can use a small window screen, or make a simple cage by stringing several pieces of 24 gauge wire vertically between two 18 gauge wires, to simulate bars in a cage. The cage should be slightly taller than the main stage and half to two-thirds the width of the stage. Be sure to bend the ends of the wires inward so that there are no sharp edges sticking out. Strips of cardboard or light wood can be used instead of wire.

Cages may also be hung from above the stage. Insert nails securely above the main stage. If the cage is tall enough, you can hang it directly on the nails; if not, attach one end of a piece of strong string to each top corner of the cage, and hang the string over the nails.

Yet another option is to have a puppeteer stand on one side of the stage and hold the cage. The drawback, of course, is that this puppeteer will be unable to operate any puppets while holding the cage and may be in the way of the other puppeteers during the chase scene in Act I.

Runaway sacks

These are not crucial props, but using them can create a charming effect in Act II. Find a few small twigs. Cut out an equal number of small pieces of fabric and place them on a table. Wrap a small wad of newspaper, paper towel, or a cotton ball in each piece of cloth, and tie securely with string or yarn. Tie each little bundle to the end of a twig.

Guitars

Draw guitars on posterboard, using a pencil. Keep the size of Omar and Brighty in mind so that the guitars are in proportion to their players. When you are satisfied with the drawings, go over them in permanent marker, decorate them as you wish, and cut them out.

Now, using a pin or point of a scissors, make holes in each guitar—one near the end of the neck and another at the far end of the guitar's body. Thread one piece of yarn through the holes on each guitar, leaving some slack, and tie the ends together. This "shoulder strap" will go around the puppet's head and suspend the guitar on the puppet's body at chest level.

Use Velcro to secure the guitars on the puppets during the third act. Sew one piece of Velcro onto the puppet's body, attaching it at a 45° angle, pointing downward from left to right. Glue a corresponding piece of Velcro horizontally along the back of the guitar. When the guitar is slung around the puppet's neck, the puppeteer should press the two pieces of Velcro together, anchoring the guitar in place, at the proper angle. (See Diagram I.33)

Microphone

For Funky's microphone, cut the shape of a small stick with a ball on top out of a piece of posterboard. Using a permanent marker or paint, color the stick black and the ball silver. Glue a thin strip of Velcro on one side of the microphone, and a corresponding piece of Velcro onto Funky's paw. Attach the microphone just before the third act and remove it afterward.

It's a good idea to make at least twice as many guitars and microphones as needed, because these props are easily bent or dropped.

Drum set

Look at a real drum set or a picture of one before you draw one onto posterboard. Decorate it, cut it out, and attach it to a stick. During Act III, the puppeteer operating Smart Alex can hold the prop from beneath, if he or she is not operating another puppet onstage. Otherwise, the bottom of the set can rest just below the edge of the stage, on nails or thumbtacks. (See Diagram I.31)

Ray's truck

Ray's truck should be cut from posterboard in the shape of a van seen from the side. It will be held from beneath on a stick, and puppets will stand behind it so it looks as if they are inside. RAY'S PET SHOP or PET PATROL may be written on the outside of the truck. There should be one front window and one rear window. The front window should be large enough to allow Ray to be seen or even to poke his head and arm out when he is driving. Funky will be seen in the rear window when Ray is taking her away at the end of Act IV.

The truck can be cumbersome to operate; it is particularly difficult to keep both Funky and Ray positioned behind their respective windows. For this reason, you may choose not to use a truck at all, in which case Ray can catch Funky in the net and pull her offstage.

The Net

Buy netting at a fabric store. Twist a long pipe cleaner or bare 24-19 gauge wire into a circle large enough for puppet to fit easily inside. Cut a circle of netting with twice the diameter of the wire circle. Fold the edge of the netting around the wire and glue it to itself all the way around. Finally, attach a piece of 19 or 18 gauge wire to the net as a handle.

Note on taping

While taping the play, be sure to leave plenty of time before and after Act III so the puppeteers can put on and take off the instruments.

Note on performing

In Act V, Slimy is supposedly tied across the stage so that Ray trips on him. Obviously, the puppet cannot be "tied"; instead, have Smart Alex pull on the Slimy puppet as the puppeteer lays him as flat and long as possible along the bottom of the stage.

Androcles and the Lion

❖❖ Androcles and the Lion

Adapted from the well-known story about two friends

Cast:
ROMAN GENERAL
ANDROCLES, *a Roman slave*
TWO SOLDIERS
LION
EMPRESS OF ROME
NARRATOR

Sets:
Rome/Colosseum
Jungle

Props:
Chariot
Thorn
Cage
Two swords

ACT I

Opening music begins. It is turned down while NARRATOR *speaks.*

NARRATOR: Welcome to our puppet theater. Our show is called *Androcles and the Lion*. The story takes place in ancient Rome, where Androcles, an unhappy slave, serves the cruel empress and the officers of her army.

(*Music is turned off. Curtain opens on the Rome/Colosseum set.* GENERAL *is already onstage.*)

GENERAL: Androcles, come here! (ANDROCLES *enters.*)

ANDROCLES: Yes, sir. I am here. How may I serve you?

GENERAL: Have you moved the pile of stones yet?

ANDROCLES: Yes, sir.

GENERAL: Have you cleaned the soldiers' quarters and washed their clothes?

ANDROCLES: I have, sir.

GENERAL: Have you fed and watered the chariot horses, brushed them, and cleaned their stables?

ANDROCLES: I have done those things, General.

GENERAL: Have you polished their harnesses?

ANDROCLES: Yes, General.

GENERAL: Not bad for a slave. I have another job for you now. Go polish the Empress' chariot and clean the cushions. She plans to ride through the streets this afternoon to take tribute and be admired. Now, go at once.

ANDROCLES: Yes, sir. I will do as good a job as the Empress' chariot deserves. (GENERAL *exits.* ANDROCLES *stands on one corner of the stage, and speaks aside to audience.*) I must escape from this place. Here, some families live as slaves, while other families live as empresses and generals. No matter what I do or how well I do it, people curse me, hit me, and order me around.

But how can I leave? There are soldiers everywhere. If I try to escape, I will be thrown to the bears or lions in the Colosseum. (*Chariot appears at other side of stage, along with* TWO SOLDIERS, *who are talking.* ANDROCLES *starts to walk over to them.*) Well, there is the chariot I have to clean. (*Short pause; suddenly*) That's it! I'll distract the guards and drive away. (*To* SOLDIERS) Excuse me, sirs.

1ST SOLDIER (*Brusquely*): Bow before us, slave. (ANDROCLES *bows.*)

ANDROCLES: I have been sent to clean this chariot for the Empress. May I enter it, please?

2ND SOLDIER: You may, lowly slave. But I hope you feel properly grateful for the honor of cleaning the Empress' chariot.

ANDROCLES: Oh yes, I do, sir.

1ST SOLDIER: And don't try any tricks. We have known slaves to try to run away. (SOLDIERS *go back to talking.* ANDROCLES *starts to work.*)

ANDROCLES *(Whispering):* Now is my chance. I'll get them to let go of the reins. *(Shouting)* Hey, look! Escaped slave! Over there! (ANDROCLES *points to one side of the stage. He runs off, as though in pursuit of someone. He is followed by soldiers.* ANDROCLES *reappears in side window.)* Over there! *(Points to other side of stage.* SOLDIERS *run across stage.* ANDROCLES *runs onstage and jumps into chariot, drives away.* SOLDIERS *run back onstage just after he disappears.)*

SOLDIERS *(Ad lib):* Wait! Stop! The dirty trickster! Sound the alarm! *Androcles* is the escaped prisoner! *(Etc. Curtain closes. During scene change,* NARRATOR *speaks.)*

NARRATOR: Androcles escaped successfully. He abandoned the chariot, freed the horse, and ran for the protection of the jungle.

*   *   *   *   *

ACT II

Scene 1

Curtain opens on the jungle set. ANDROCLES *comes onstage.*

ANDROCLES: I am weary and hungry, but at least I will be safe from the soldiers for a while. *(Short pause)* That cave over there will be cool and dark—a perfect place for me to rest. (ANDROCLES *enters cave.)*

LION: Raaahhhhr! (ANDROCLES *runs out of cave, trembling. Growling and roaring are heard from cave as* ANDROCLES *runs offstage and then peeks back onstage.* LION *comes out of cave, growling and shouting.)* Leave me alone! Go away!

ANDROCLES *(Trembling):* I apologize. I did not realize this cave belonged to you.

LION: I will not kill you this time. But please do not ever come back! (LION *starts to go inside.)*

ANDROCLES: Please wait a moment, Lion. You are limping, and I see something sticking out of your paw. It looks like a thorn. It must be extremely painful! Please let me remove it for you, and then I will be on my way.

LION: Do not come any closer! I will not let you trap me and take me to the Colosseum. I will eat you first!

ANDROCLES (*Laughing*): Why would *I* trap you? And why would I possibly want to take you to Rome? I just escaped from that city, and I hope never to return.

LION: I have never met an honest human. Stay where you are!

ANDROCLES (*Slowly approaching* LION): I just want to take out your thorn. See, I'm coming very slowly, very carefully.

LION (*Threateningly*): Grrahharr! (ANDROCLES *reaches* LION *and takes hold of thorn, then quickly removes it.*) Ow!

ANDROCLES: There! Now, you will feel much better. (*There is a slight pause, as* ANDROCLES *turns to exit.*) Goodbye.

LION: Wait! You really did just want to help me—and you are unarmed. You must stay awhile as my guest, for you are the first human I have met whom I can trust.

ANDROCLES: Let's consider ourselves friends, then.

LION: And whatever I can do for you, I will. Now, please rest here for a few days. (*They shake hands. Optional: Music in background during narration.*)

NARRATOR: So, Androcles and the lion became friends. Androcles tended the lion's wound and told him about Rome. And the lion taught Androcles how to survive in the jungle. Eventually, however, Androcles knew that he had to move on or he would be captured by the soldiers sent out after him.

LION: Grrr! I hear soldiers in armor coming. Their blood-smell makes my whiskers curl. You had better run quickly. And I will hide in my cave so that they do not trap me.

ANDROCLES: Goodbye, Lion. Thank you for your hospitality.

LION: I thank *you*, brave human. Good luck and farewell! (ANDROCLES *exits.* LION *goes into cave.* GENERAL *and* SOLDIERS *appear.*)

GENERAL (*Pointing to cave*): Aha! A cave where that slave is probably hiding! You two go in, and bring him back in chains. (SOLDIERS *go into cave, then after a moment come running out, screaming, as big roar is heard from* LION. *All three run offstage. Then* SOLDIERS *appear in side window.*) Well, I was wrong. Androcles is not the one in the cave. But the Empress will be thrilled if we send her back such a huge, beautiful lion.

She can use him in the Colosseum to fight other animals or to kill slaves. Let's fix a trap for it. *(Curtain)*

* * * * *

Scene 2

The trap is set up offstage during the following narration.

NARRATOR: The soldiers did set a trap for the lion; once again, the general sent his two men into the cave, this time to bait the lion. *(Curtain opens. Chase music begins.* SOLDIERS *come running out of cave, chased by the roaring* LION. *They run around a little, then* LION *is caught in the falling cage. Music stops.)*

GENERAL *(Pleased):* Wonderful! We'll send the lion back with guards tomorrow morning. Then we will continue our search for Androcles. *(Curtain)*

* * * * *

Scene 3

The cage is removed during the following narration.

NARRATOR: The lion was sent away to Rome, miserable and angry. Meanwhile, Androcles was wandering through the jungle, trying to hide from the soldiers. Eventually, he stopped to rest. *(Curtain opens, still on jungle set, with* ANDROCLES *lying asleep onstage.* SOLDIERS *and* GENERAL *enter.)*

GENERAL: The slave! Get him! *(*SOLDIERS *run toward* ANDROCLES. AN-DROCLES *jumps up, knocking them over and grabbing sword from one of them. While* SOLDIERS *are on the ground,* GENERAL *comes forward with his sword and fights with* ANDROCLES. *Meanwhile,* SOLDIERS *get up and sneak behind* ANDROCLES. *They grab his arms so he drops the sword, and restrain him.)*

1ST SOLDIER: We have him, General.

2ND SOLDIER: What should we do with him?

GENERAL: Bring him in chains to Rome. Soon, he will die! *(Curtain. Sad music is heard for several seconds, then turned down for the narration. During scene change,* NARRATOR *speaks.)*

NARRATOR: Androcles was brought by the soldiers to a small, gloomy jail cell. He sat there for days, thinking how happy his friend must be in the jungle. He thought of other lions, who would be starved and then sent into the Colosseum to kill him. One day, guards came to his cell and led him to the loud Colosseum, where the Empress was opening the games.

* * * * *

ACT III

Curtain opens on Rome/Colosseum set. The noise of trumpets and a crowd can be heard. EMPRESS *appears in a side window. The noise recedes to the background.*

EMPRESS: Release the slave and the fierce beast! Let the games begin! (*Laughs with excitement.* ANDROCLES *walks out, looking scared.* LION *comes charging out.*)

ANDROCLES (*Terrified*): Help! (*Short chase scene on stage. After ten to fifteen seconds, the two come face to face.*)

LION (*Shocked*): It's you!

ANDROCLES (*Relieved*): I'm saved!

LION: My friend, Androcles! (*They hug.*)

EMPRESS: What are they doing?! Hugging! That lion we've been starving for two weeks should be brutally attacking the slave! I can't understand it! Disperse the crowds, guards. Slave! Slave! Come here at once. (AN-DROCLES *and* LION *walk toward* EMPRESS. ANDROCLES *has his arm around* LION. *They bow before* EMPRESS, *who is surprised and angry.*) Just what is the meaning of this! My new prize lion is acting like your puppy dog!

ANDROCLES: Imperial Majesty, this lion *is* as gentle as a pet. We are friends. We met in the jungle when I ran away from this city. The lion had a thorn in his paw and I removed it for him. He has shown his gratitude by taking care of me in the jungle, and now, by sparing my life.

EMPRESS (*Impressed*): Incredible! I have never heard of such a thing! Androcles, I will free you and make you my imperial lion tamer. You will be rich with slaves and money, and everyone will admire you.

ANDROCLES: No, thank you, your highness. I could not stay here and have slaves of my own. Either kill me—or let me return to the jungle with this friendly lion.

EMPRESS *(Shaking her head; perplexed):* I cannot understand you, but I fear the power you must have. You are free to go where you please—and so is this lion, as long as you are with him. *(Sighs in exasperation)* I will supply you with whatever you need. *(*EMPRESS *exits.* ANDROCLES *and* LION *stand together on stage, facing audience.)*

NARRATOR: And so Androcles and the lion went back to the jungle together—and they lived happily there for the rest of their lives. *(Triumphant music begins.* ANDROCLES *and* LION *wave to audience.)*

NARRATOR, ANDROCLES, *and* LION: *The End!* *(Music fades. Curtain)*

Production Notes
ANDROCLES AND THE LION

Puppets

The characters in *Androcles and the Lion* are well-suited to be played by hand puppets with papier-mâché heads and cloth bodies.

Androcles

Androcles wears simple tunic, easily made from a single piece of white cloth over brown for his arms and legs.

General and Soldiers

Soldiers wear identical uniforms and helmets, but look slightly different. Perhaps one could be made with a long head and the other with a round head. The helmets can be made as one piece with the papier-mâché heads or made out of construction paper or cloth and tied, stapled, or glued onto the soldiers' heads. The general's costume should be somewhat different from the soldiers'. His clothes or helmet can have special markings, such as stars or ribbons. All three should wear swords (see notes on props below).

Lion

You may make the lion with a papier-mâché head and cloth body. The lion's head should be carefully shaped so that it is rounded with pointed ears and a broad face. It can be painted a golden brown color, with brown eyes and a black nose. Whiskers can be made from broom or other straw or from wire, and glued to the face. The lion's body can be made out of furry golden or tawny-colored cloth. Use matching cloth with a slightly different colored tuft of brown fabric or yarn at the end to make a tail. Make the lion's mane by attaching many short pieces of yarn to a thick strip of heavy cloth, and sewing or stapling the cloth around the lion's face.

Empress

The Empress wears a gown of shiny fabric, a crown, and jewelry, if you like.

Sets

Since there are only two sets necessary for *Androcles and the Lion,* this play is faster and simpler to perform than most other shows.

Colosseum

The first and last acts take place in Rome. Of course, the last act requires a depiction of the Colosseum since all the action takes place there, but for the first act the Colosseum set will also be sufficient to set the city scene. Otherwise, a set showing a castle and stables could be used in Act I.

To make the Colosseum, you can use any color posterboard, but brown, pink, red, or gray would best suggest the stone from which it was made. A coliseum is like a round or oval ice-skating arena. Imagine that you are standing at the center of the arena. In front of you, there is open space, then a curved section of seats. This is the same way you can paint or draw the set: The foreground will be the empty arena; the higher parts—about half the set—will be the rows of seats curving around. You can look for a picture of the Colosseum in the library to give you a clearer idea of how it looks.

Jungle

Most of the play's action takes place with the jungle set as the background. It is consequently a very important set, worth creating with great care. A light green background is best; decorate the set densely with palm trees, bushes, tropical flowers and plants, stones, monkeys, birds, a swamp, or anything else you like.

The one part of the set that is essential is the lion's cave, which should be off toward one side. Cut an arch in the set. Make sure the hole is large enough for the lion and the soldiers to go through. You have created a cave; the black background cloth of your puppet stage will make it look as if the cave is dark inside. (See Diagram 1.28.)

Props

Horse and chariot

Draw a horse and chariot on white posterboard, using a pencil. When you are satisfied with it, retrace it with black marker. Decorate it with markers and glitter. Cut the prop out carefully, making sure to leave two large pieces of posterboard along the bottom, one piece under the chariot wheel, and the other under the back legs of the horse. These will be the supports of the prop, to which handles (made of dowel rods, straight twigs, or thick paint brushes) should be attached with masking tape. (See Diagram I.30)

Thorn

A large toothpick works perfectly for the thorn. Otherwise, use a twig.

Cage

Cut rectangular sections along one long side of a shoe box, making sure not to cut all the way to the edges. The side with the strips cut out will be the front of the cage. The cage will be held by a puppeteer offstage and will come down from above to trap the lion. Attach a dowel rod or stick on the back side of the cage, near the top, for the puppeteer to hold.

You may also make the cage out of twisted 19-18 gauge wire.

Simpler still is to substitute a net for the cage. See instructions for making a net on page 80.

Swords

Draw a sword and hilt on posterboard. It should be the appropriate size for a puppet to hold with two hands during the fight. Decorate it with permanent markers, then cut it out. It can be attached to a puppet's side or hand with Velcro.

Notes on taping

Sword fight

When taping the fight scene (Act II, Scene 3), two knives may be clanged together to simulate the sounds of a sword fight. Read the stage directions carefully before recording this section, so that you can insert shouts and sword-clangs at appropriate moments. It is a good idea for the actors doing the voices of Androcles and the General to act out the fight scene as they record it.

Crowd sound effect

To simulate the noise of the crowd in the Colosseum (Act III), you may use a recording of cheers on a live concert album or a sound effects record. Otherwise, the members of the cast can simulate the noise by making a "ha" sound with their mouths opened wide.

Notes on performance

Entering and exiting through the cave

Make sure to go completely in or out. Try not to hit the jungle set as you move, or the illusion of space will be lost.

Trapping the lion

The puppeteer who works the General should be the one to lower the cage, since the General puppet is offstage at the time.

Staging of Act III

The Empress should remain in a side window the entire scene. This will make it appear as though she is in a special box or seat and not standing in the arena with Androcles and the Lion.

Danger in Pleasant Woods

◆◆ Danger in Pleasant Woods

Nature plays a starring role

Cast:
ALVIN ICHABOD, *a land developer*
STRIPE, *a skunk*
MRS. PLEASANT, *an old woman*
MR. PLEASANT, *an old man*
JUNE, *a juniper bush*
MAGIC SPIRIT OF THE WOOD, *an ancient tree*
NARRATOR

Sets:
The Pleasants' house
Pleasant Woods
Magic Woods
Ichabod's home

Props:
Large sack
Deed
Vial of potion
Net
Flowers

ACT I

Opening music is heard. After several seconds, it is turned down while NARRATOR *speaks.*

NARRATOR: Hi, everybody! Today's show is called *Danger in Pleasant Woods*. We hope you enjoy it. *(Music is briefly turned up, and then off. Curtain opens to show the Pleasants' house.* ICHABOD *is holding onto a bag in which* STRIPE *is trapped.* STRIPE *struggles in the bag.)*

ICHABOD *(Calling toward house):* Open up! Come out of there, right now!

MR. *and* MRS. PLEASANT *(From offstage):* What is it? Who's there? *(MR. and* MRS. PLEASANT *walk on, gasping when they see bag.)*

MR. PLEASANT: Oh, no! He's got one of the animals! *(STRIPE struggles.)*

MRS. PLEASANT: Help!

ICHABOD: Now, don't call for help, or you'll never see this skunk again! Or any of the animals from your forest!

MR. PLEASANT *(Upset):* What do you want with us? We told you we didn't want to sell our forest. We won't let you tear down the trees.

MRS. PLEASANT: Or bulldoze the mountains.

MR. PLEASANT: Or kill the animals.

ICHABOD: Once you sign this deed saying the land belongs to me, I'll do whatever I want.

MRS. PLEASANT *(In disbelief):* You wouldn't really destroy this forest and build a city, would you?

ICHABOD *(Short pause, then sweetly):* You know, you're right, Mrs. Pleasant. I wouldn't do a thing like that. I was just afraid that you would not trust my good intentions if I told you the truth. You see, I just want to take care of all the nice animals and plants, and, if you excuse my saying so, I think I can protect this beautiful unspoiled land better than, well, old people like you. *(MR. and* MRS. PLEASANT *look at one another.)*

MRS. PLEASANT *(Hesitating):* We have kept it for so long . . .

MR. PLEASANT *(Slowly):* Well, if you promise . . .

ICHABOD *(Quickly):* Oh, I promise I'll never touch any of this forest or build a single thing. So, just sign this deed and I'll release this adorable skunk right back into the woods.

MR. PLEASANT: I think we should do it, Ella. He did give his word.

MRS. PLEASANT: I think you're right. *(They sign the deed.)*

ICHABOD *(Evilly):* Aha! You fools! You have one week—do you hear me, one week—to move, before I bulldoze your house and the rest of the forest. Finally, my newest condominium complex, "Pine Free," will be built!

MRS. PLEASANT *(Upset):* You lied to us. Give us back the deed! Please!

ICHABOD: Never! Ha-ha-ha! *(There is a short chase scene, during which the following lines are spoken.)*

MR. PLEASANT: Help! Help!

MRS. PLEASANT: Please give it back!

ICHABOD: Ha-ha-ha-ha-ha! *(ICHABOD exits with deed. PLEASANTS, out of breath, reappear center stage.)*

MR. PLEASANT: I'm sorry, Ella. I trusted him. Now we no longer have a home.

MRS. PLEASANT: I trusted him, too, dear. The terrible part is not what will become of us, but what will become of the forest. Let's go inside and plan what to do next. *(PLEASANTS put their arms around each other and walk offstage. As they walk off, STRIPE wriggles out of the bag, looks after them sadly, and then runs offstage. Curtain)*

* * * * *

ACT II

Curtain opens on Pleasant Woods. JUNE *is on stage.* STRIPE *enters quickly.*

STRIPE *(Slightly out of breath):* June, wake up! What are we going to do?

JUNE: Calm down, Stripe. What's wrong?

STRIPE: What's wrong?! *What's wrong?!* That land developer, Alvin Ichabod, caught me and put me in a bag. He threatened to hurt me if the Pleasants didn't sign over the forest to him. Then, he told them that if he owned the forest, he wouldn't really tear it down, but would protect all the trees and animals. But he lied to them and tricked them into signing a deed! Now he owns the forest, and he *is* going to tear it down!

JUNE: Oh, that Ichabod! If I could move, I would walk right up to him and get that deed back. If only bushes had real legs.

STRIPE: Maybe *I* could do something, June.

JUNE: You have to, before it's too late. Go to the Magic Spirit of the Woods and ask for help.

STRIPE: How do I do that?

JUNE: Walk to the end of the forest and say these words over and over:

Magic Spirit, please hear me!
Magic Spirit, send me to the Magic Wood!
Magic Spirit, please see me!
I call upon the strength of the good!

STRIPE: I'm scared.

JUNE: You can do it, Stripe. We need you.

STRIPE *(Bravely)*: All right, June. I'll try. Goodbye. *(He exits slowly.)*

JUNE: Goodbye, Stripe—and good luck! (STRIPE *appears in side window as curtain closes.*)

STRIPE: Magic Spirit, please hear me!
Magic Spirit, send me to the Magic Wood!
Magic Spirit, please see me!
I call upon the strength of the good!

(Dramatic music is heard as STRIPE *disappears from window and set is changed.)*

*   *   *   *   *

ACT III

Curtain opens on Magic Woods. The music fades out. STRIPE *enters.*

MAGIC SPIRIT *(Offstage; in thundering voice)*: Who has called upon my powers? *(Thumping of footsteps can be heard as* MAGIC SPIRIT *slowly appears on stage.)*

STRIPE *(Nervously)*: It is I, Magic Spirit—Stripe, the skunk, from Pleasant Woods.

MAGIC SPIRIT: I have been watching the danger in Pleasant Woods. I am sorry, but *(With a sigh)* I cannot come to help you. There is even greater danger in the Black Forest of Germany, demanding my full attention.

STRIPE *(Disappointed)*: You were our only hope. Our forest will be destroyed!

MAGIC SPIRIT: No, there is something that you can do yourself. *(Reaches offstage for net)* If you can catch Ichabod in this magic net, my powers will transport him to a large city far away. He will never come near your forest again.

STRIPE: How can I do that alone? He'll catch me again!

MAGIC SPIRIT: There is a very brave young shrub in your woods—your friend, June. She will help you.

98

STRIPE: But June cannot move!

MAGIC SPIRIT: She cannot move now, but when you give her this magic potion, she will be able to go anywhere she wishes. *(*MAGIC SPIRIT *leans offstage to get magic vial, which she gives to* STRIPE.*)* Now, close your eyes. When you open them again, you will find yourself back in Pleasant Woods. I wish you luck, little one. *(There are thumping sounds as* MAGIC SPIRIT *walks offstage.* STRIPE *covers his eyes. Curtain closes as dramatic music begins again.)*

*   *   *   *   *

ACT IV

The music stops. Curtain opens on Pleasant Woods, with STRIPE *at center stage, still covering his eyes.* JUNE *is at one side.* STRIPE *uncovers his eyes and jumps in surprise.*

STRIPE: Ah! How did I get here? I thought I was in the Magic Woods!

JUNE: The Magic Spirit sent you back. *(Urgently)* Stripe, we have no time to waste. Please tell me what the Spirit said.

STRIPE: Well, the Spirit is going to help us, but we have to do our part, too. After you can walk, we'll leave for Ichabod's at once. I will tell you what we must do as we go.

JUNE *(Shocked):* What? Did you say *walk?*

STRIPE: Yes, the Spirit gave me a magic potion that will make you able to move.

JUNE *(Excited):* You mean I'm really going to walk?

STRIPE: That's what the Spirit said. Here you go! *(*STRIPE *leans offstage and is quickly handed the magic vial. He walks around* JUNE, *shaking the vial near the ground. Dynamic music begins, as* JUNE *starts to move and twist, then leaps out of her place.)*

JUNE *(Shouting happily):* I can move! I can jump! I can walk! Hooray! We can save the woods. Let's go! *(*JUNE *runs offstage, followed by* STRIPE.*)*

STRIPE: Wait for me! *(Curtain)*

*   *   *   *   *

ACT V

Curtain opens on ICHABOD's *home and surroundings.* ICHABOD *walks onstage, holding deed.*

ICHABOD: This is the greatest day of my life! *(Spreading arms wide)* Soon, all this will be one huge city. The woods will no longer stand between my house and my condominiums over there. *(Points offstage)* No more wild animals or stupid old trees! *(Short pause.* ICHABOD *yawns.)* I'm tired. I won't let go of this deed for a minute, but I think I'll take a nap here in the sun. It's not as good as an artificial sunlamp, but it will have to do. *(Holding the deed,* ICHABOD *settles down against one corner of the stage. He sighs contentedly, then starts to snore. There are a few seconds of snoring, then* JUNE *and* STRIPE *peek around the opposite side of the stage and jump back. They peek around again.)*

JUNE: O.K., here I go. *(*JUNE *creeps forward and then stops suddenly and stands still, as* ICHABOD *jumps to his feet. Meanwhile* STRIPE, *who has been peeking out from backstage, draws back.)*

ICHABOD: Who's there? I must have been dreaming. *(He settles back down.* JUNE *creeps forward another step or two. She freezes again, as* ICHABOD *awakens.* STRIPE *peeks out and back as he did the last time.)* What's that? *(Shakes head)* What's wrong with me? There is nothing here but me, my house, and a stupid little bush. I hate plants! I'll have it torn up, first thing tomorrow. Now, I'll just relax. *(*JUNE *pauses, then, as* ICH-ABOD *begins to snore again,* JUNE *darts forward and grabs the deed from his hand.* ICHABOD *jumps up.)* Come back here! Give that to me! *(There is a chase scene with music,* STRIPE *following* ICHABOD *following* JUNE. *Eventually,* JUNE, *who has dropped the deed backstage, comes running back toward* ICHABOD, *this time with the net.* ICHABOD *turns and sees* STRIPE *right behind him. Whoosh! The net comes down over him.* JUNE *and* STRIPE *hold it down together.* ICHABOD *is frantic.)* Let me out of here!

STRIPE *and* JUNE *(Together):*

> Oh, Great Spirit, wise and good,
> Please take Ichabod from Pleasant Woods.

(There is a rumbling sound and then ICHABOD *vanishes.)*

STRIPE: Yay! He's gone!

JUNE: Great work, Stripe! We'll never need to worry about him again. Now, let's take the deed back to the Pleasants. *(Curtain. The scene change is accompanied by happy music.)*

* * * * *

ACT VI

Curtain opens on Pleasant Woods. PLEASANTS, STRIPE, *and* JUNE *enter, holding hands, hugging, and patting each other on the back.*

JUNE: Hooray! The woods are saved!

MRS. PLEASANT: I don't know what we would have done without you two. We had already packed to leave.

MR. PLEASANT: And you've saved the whole forest. Thank you, thank you!

STRIPE: You've done all of us a favor by keeping our home safe for us all these years. We're glad we could help.

MRS. PLEASANT: And from this day forward, the forest will be more important than ever to us, because the Magic Spirit has given us the power to talk to the trees and animals we love. *(Happy music begins again.)*

NARRATOR: And so the forest grew ever more beautiful and magical. From that day forward, there was no end to its surprises. *(Flowers pop up immediately. Music gets louder.)*

ALL: *The End!* *(Curtain. Music fades.)*

Production Notes
DANGER IN PLEASANT WOODS

Puppets

Mr. and Mrs. Pleasant

The puppets for the Pleasants can be made with papier-mâché heads and cloth bodies. The cloth bodies should be designed with simple clothing—overalls for Mr. Pleasant, plain dress for Mrs. Pleasant.

Ichabod

This puppet, too, can best be made with a papier-mâché head and cloth body. A trench coat, dark suit, or silky shirt and chain would be appropriate costumes.

Stripe

The skunk puppet can be made of black furry cloth or a pair of men's large black socks. (Socks of a different color can be dyed with black fabric dye.) Consult the directions for making cloth and sock puppets with arms in Part I.

Make a tail out of a black tennis sock (without a pompom). Put your arm inside the puppet and note the place on the outside of the puppet above your wrist. (If a sock is used for the skunk's body, this will be near the heel.) This will be the point at which you will attach the tail. Now, remove your arm, and place the tennis sock, opening downward, on top of the puppet. Sew only the top part of the sock to the puppet's body, so the rest of the tail hangs free.

Glue white furry cloth or thick white yarn down the back of the puppet and on the underside of the tail to represent stripes. Bead eyes can be bought at a fabric store. To make ears, sew half-circles of felt or other fabric onto the head.

June

The juniper bush can be made out of dark green cloth. Cover a person's fist or a baseball with the cloth to get an idea of where to gather the cloth for the bush's body. Use elastic or thread to make the gather, but do not cut off the remaining cloth; it will hide the puppeteer's arm when June becomes mobile and is raised up and down as she moves about the stage.

Attach eyes to one side of the gathered fabric. (Because this part of the puppet will move around quite a bit, it's better to use eyes that can be sewn on rather than glued.) Now, cut leaves out of felt or cardboard, and sew them on at varying angles all over the front and back of the puppet. If you are giving only one performance, you may choose to use real leaves pasted on in abundance; you should realize that some will crumple, wilt, or fall off during the performance.

June can also be made out of a dark green sock decorated with leaves and eyes.

A third possibility is to make June a rod puppet. Though this does not allow the flexibility of movement that a cloth puppet does, it may look more like a real bush. Dip a dish brush made out of plastic bristles or a sponge into green dye or paint, and let it dry. Attach eyes and/or leaves, if you wish. Make a tube out of green fabric, attach the top of it to the top of the handle, and let it hang down far enough to hide the handle and the puppeteer's hand.

The Magic Spirit

The Magic Spirit in this play is a beautiful old tree, neither male nor female (though you may choose to make the Spirit a bird, a flower, an owl, or even a stone).

The tree can be made out of a green work glove and a large brown sock or tube of fabric. Sew the fabric to the inside bottom of the glove (so the stitching does not show). Be sure there is enough room all up and down the puppet for the puppeteer's arm and hand to get in and out without difficulty. Now, attach real twigs, or brown felt cut in the shape of branches, to the fingers of the glove, radiating from the palm. A few short "branches" may radiate out below the thumb and little finger to the sides of the palm. Using glitter and leaves made of fabric, cardboard, or construction paper, decorate the tree. Try to make it look special; remember—it is a magical tree. Make sure it looks clearly different from June.

Sets

The Pleasants' house

Paint a small, neat house, perhaps with a front porch, on yellow, pink, sky blue, or any other light-color posterboard. Around it, there may be grass, trees, a garden, and/or a path to the house. Leave room for a blue sky and puffy clouds. The Pleasants' house should be a peaceful, quiet-looking place.

Pleasant Woods

Make these woods dense with trees. Here and there, you may make stones, bushes, or flowers. Leave a clearing in the foreground where June will stand.

The Magic Woods

It is important that this set be distinct from the set for Pleasant Woods. You may choose to make it darker, with or without a moon. Owls, or just eyes, may peek from trees. It may enhance the set to make strong color contrasts and surprises. Fantastical flowers may grow here and there; imaginary animals of vivid pink or other colors may move among the trees.

Ichabod's home

Ichabod's home should be very different from the Pleasants' house, and should reflect Ichabod's taste for artificial things. It might not be a house at all, but a large building, a condominium, or a glass skyscraper. Remember: He does not like trees, plants, or animals.

To give an idea of where Ichabod lives, you may want to make his home on one side of the set with part of a smoky city on the other side. In between could lie a wooded area representing Pleasant Woods, which (as Ichabod says in Act V), "stand between my house and my condominiums over there."

Props

Sack

The sack may be made out of white, brown, or gold cloth or rough burlap-like fabric. Cut a rectangle of fabric. Now, make a tube out of the fabric, either sewing it or using safety pins. Tie the top of the tube with a piece of yarn or string. Make sure that the tube is large enough to cover the puppeteer's arm when he or she is wearing Stripe. Now, you have a sack to fit over the puppet, which makes it look as though the skunk is completely inside it. It will be easy for the puppeteer operating Stripe to remove the sack with his or her free hand during the chase scene in Act I.

Deed

Cut a small (about 2″ by 2½″) rectangle of white posterboard; the puppets must be able to carry it easily, even as they are running around on the stage. Scribble lines of "writing" on one side of the deed. On the reverse side, write, "Deed to Pleasant Woods."

As with all small, hand-held props, I suggest making three or four copies of it, especially if you are doing more than one performance. Keep copies on either side of the stage during the performance. If the deed slips out of a puppet's hand, he can quickly move to the side of the stage and be handed a replacement.

Magic vial

One simple way to make this prop is to cut a bottle shape out of posterboard. Paint the lower portion a vibrant color—blue or red, for instance—to make it look as though there is fluid in the vial. If you wish, you may add glitter to the painted part.

The vial can also be made out of a small test tube, filled with glitter and securely closed with a rubber stopper, or you can cover the outside of an egg timer or small test tube with colored glitter or glitter paint.

Net

To make a net, follow the instructions on page 80.

Flowers

It makes a nice surprise at the end of the play if flowers pop up as though they have grown instantly. Make flowers using bright tissue paper or facial tissue attached to wire or pipe cleaners. You may also buy a few inexpensive silk flowers at a flower or craft store. Bind the stems together so that they can easily be held in one person's hand and pop up together at the right moment.

Jody's Journey

◆◆ **Jody's Journey**

Adventure on another planet

Cast:
JODY, *a girl from Earth*
ERALK, *a scholar and leader of Petrolon*
ZORP ⎫
TWERP ⎬ *Petrolonese*
TWO SNATRONS, *vicious creatures*
NARRATOR
VOICE OF MOTHER

Sets:
Bright side of Petrolon
Dangerous side of Petrolon

Props:
Spaceship
Magic wand
Volcano
Power stone
Ring

ACT I

Music can be heard. After a short time, the music is turned down.

NARRATOR: Welcome! Today we are proud to present the puppet show, *Jody's Journey*. It is a story about a brave girl who travels to a strange planet and saves the inhabitants from eternal darkness. Her mission is a difficult one, so please listen carefully—she might need your help. *(Music is turned louder for several seconds, then turned down.* NARRATOR *speaks calmly.)* It is nighttime. Jody is asleep in her bed at home. *(Abruptly, in dramatic tone of voice)* Then, suddenly she is being hurled through time and space. While asleep, she spins through light years to the planet of Petrolon. *(Music is again turned louder for several seconds, then fades out. Curtain opens on bright side of Petrolon.* JODY *is asleep on the ground.* ZORP *and* TWERP *appear, and begin walking around her, whispering, poking her, trying to figure out who and what she is. Eerie or suspenseful music can be heard in the background.* ZORP *shakes* JODY. JODY *yawns and starts to stretch. The music stops.)*

JODY *(Still half-asleep):* O.K. Mom, I'll be down in a minute. You know, I had the weirdest dream that I traveled to another planet and there were all these Martians or something looking at me and wondering who I was. But then you woke me up. *(*JODY *yawns again. She sits up and sees* ZORP *and* TWERP.*)* Mom?! Oh, no! Help! *(*ZORP *and* TWERP *run away.* JODY *stands, rubbing her eyes.* ZORP *and* TWERP *come back on stage slowly. During following conversation,* ZORP *and* TWERP *alternately peek out around the corners of the stage; appear in side windows, looking at* JODY; *approach her cautiously to touch her, and then run away at once.)*

ZORP: Drrp! Zrrrawraw tsip! EEEaaaa!

TWERP: Trrraa! *(Calls off)* Eralk! *(*ERALK *runs on.* ZORP *and* TWERP *exit.)*

ERALK: Ralfaroop! *(Looking at her)* You appear to be a child from the planet Earth. Am I correct in that assumption?

JODY *(Terrified):* Well—well, yes. You speak English?

ERALK: Yes. I am Eralk, Petrolon's language scholar. I study the languages of other planets. *(Pause)* At least I did, before The Tragedy.

JODY: What tragedy? *(Shakes head)* I must be imagining this. This *must* be a joke.

ERALK: If this is a joke, then it is being played on us, too. I have no time to talk. We must figure out what to do about The Tragedy and reclaiming the stone.

JODY *(Bewildered):* What are you talking about? I don't know what you mean when you say "The Tragedy." Am I really on another planet?

ERALK: You are on the planet Petrolon, young person. But I do not have time to explain to you about The Tragedy or our planet. You will not be able to help, and besides, you are in great danger here. You should return to Earth at once.

JODY: All right, I'm ready.

ERALK: Well, travel safely. Goodbye. *(He starts to exit.)*

JODY *(Frantically):* Wait! Aren't you going to send me back to Earth?

ERALK: Oh, I see. You cannot travel back by yourself, can you?

JODY *(Shaking her head):* No.

ERALK: Well, that is a dilemna, since I cannot possibly send you until we reclaim our power stone. *(Crying)* Tsk, tsk. Zaarrrp!

JODY: What power stone? *(Patting him on the back)* Please don't cry.

ERALK *(Resignedly):* Well, I might as well tell you. There is nothing we can do now, anyway. As I said, this planet is called Petrolon, and we—Zorp, Twerp, and I—are leaders of the Petrolonese people. We are peaceful people, and we used to be happy, until the Terrastadon came. The Terrastadon is what you on Earth would call a terrible vicious beast from outer space. He stole our power stone, which is the source of our light, energy, and ability to stay at peace. He has taken it to the other side of the planet. Already, that side has become dark and empty. Cruel space-beasts, like the snatrons, have come to live there. Soon these beasts will come here, too, and we will be powerless against them without our stone. We cannot even flee from the planet—or send you home—without the power stone. This is our tragic situation, Earthling.

JODY: You can call me Jody.

ERALK: Jody.

JODY: But doesn't the monster have any weaknesses? There must be some way you can get the power stone back from him.

ERALK: No, Jody. The Terrastadon has many arms, and many ears, and he is very sensitive to sound. It drives him crazy! If we start to come near him, he hears us and chases us. And even worse than his arms, with their claws and suction cups, is his gruesome mouth, which shoots poison!

JODY *(Cringing):* Oh, how awful! The Terrastadon sounds very frightening *(Hesitates, then continues firmly),* but my parents tell me never to give up. One has to face her enemies. I will try to take back the power stone.

ERALK: You cannot do that!

JODY: Well, I can't let your people be killed—and I must return home. I miss it already. Please let me go.

ERALK: All right, Jody, but I will give you something to help you. *(Calls to*

ZORP *and* TWERP*)* Zorp, Twerp, arrreeeeebobbosheedontemporasleen!
*(*ZORP *and* TWERP *run onstage with magic wand.* ERALK *motions to*
JODY *to take wand, which she does.)* Jody, here is Zequinon—what you
would call a magic wand. If you concentrate all your strength into it and
point it straight at your enemies, they will disappear. I warn you,
though, it will not do any good against the Terrastadon.

JODY: Thank you, Eralk. *(She turns to go.)*

ERALK: Do not go so quickly, Jody. If you walk back there *(He points.),* you
will find a spaceship that was recharged just before the stone was taken.
The ship is programmed to take you to the other side of the planet. It has
just enough power for one trip.

JODY: Well, I'll do all I can. Goodbye! *(She exits. Petrolonese wave, say
goodbye in their language, then exit. Curtain. Music begins. Spaceship
can be seen flying above stage. The ship disappears as the music stops.)*

* * * * *

ACT II

*Curtain opens on dangerous side of planet. The power stone rests on one
side of the stage, next to volcano.* JODY *enters from other side, holding
magic wand and whistling.*

JODY *(Nervously):* There. I think I've whistled everything I know and a lot
I've made up. For some reason, it makes me feel a little safer. *(She
whistles a little more. Suddenly,* TWO SNATRONS *appear, one jumping
from high up on one side of the stage, the other appearing from underneath, right beside* JODY.

1ST SNATRON: Grrraab herr! *(*SNATRONS *chase* JODY *back and forth across
stage. They grab her and pull on her. She frees herself.)*

JODY *(To herself):* I've got to use the magic wand. Point it straight.
(Louder) Now, there! *(*JODY *touches* 1ST SNATRON *with magic wand and
it disappears at once with a little noise.)* And there! *(*2ND SNATRON
disappears with a noise, as JODY *touches it with wand.* JODY *sits,
slightly out of breath.)* Those must have been snatrons. I read about
them in the spaceship. I'm lucky I had the magic wand, but I think I
should leave it here. I'll need both hands for the Terrastadon! The talking
computer map in the ship said that he was hiding out right behind that
volcano. I'll climb it very quietly and catch a glimpse of him. *(*JODY *gets*

up and begins to climb volcano. *Meanwhile,* TERRASTADON *appears in side window, gurgling.* JODY *slowly climbs up one side of volcano, whistling to herself. She gets to top, sees* TERRASTADON, *then slips down other side of volcano.)* Oh, no! I'm slipping! *(*TERRASTADON *sees her and starts chasing her, gurgling and squirting poison. They have a fairly long chase scene using side windows.* JODY *just manages to escape back over volcano.* TERRASTADON *exits.)* What will I do? He almost caught me! But I must go back. I have to find a way to get the power stone. Now, what did Eralk tell me about him? *(Short pause)* He said the Terrastadon shoots poison, and he has big claws—*I'll* say he has big claws!

TERRASTADON *(From offstage):* I can hear you!

JODY *(Exasperated):* And he hates noise! *(Suddenly encouraged)* Hey, that's it! He hates noise! He hates it so much that if I could make enough noise, he might disappear.

This is what I'll do. I'll climb quietly over the volcano. Then, I'll come charging down the other side, yelling at the top of my lungs. I know he'll start chasing me. But if I can make enough noise, maybe I can make *him* run away from *me. (Suddenly disappointed)* But how can I possibly do that by myself? I'll get poisoned unless I have help. *(To audience)* Listen! If anybody on Earth knows I'm here, make some noise! Come on, clap, whistle, shout as loud as you can! I mean *you* out there. Is anybody watching? Let's practice! *(Clapping and shouting)* Louder! Louder! *(She stops clapping, pauses)* I hear something. Yea! I just heard some noise coming from Earth! *(*TERRASTADON *appears in side window, gurgling and shooting poison.)* Now, I need everyone to be very, very quiet. Don't say anything. Sh-h-h! I'm sneaking up the volcano, and when I get to the top I need everyone to help me by screaming and stomping and making noise. I'm climbing, quietly, quietly. *(*JODY *climbs volcano. Suddenly)* Now! *(*JODY *yells and claps.* TERRASTADON *chases her, shooting poison as she runs.)* I'll get you, you terrible Terrastadon. I'll teach you to steal the Petrolonese stone! How do you like all this noise? Hear it? I hear some sympathetic people shouting all the way from Earth!

TERRASTADON: *Eeeee!* I can't bear it! *(*TERRASTADON *runs off, gurgling and protesting.)*

JODY *(Happily):* Yea! We did it! We made enough noise to send that Terrastadon away for good. Now I'll get back to the bright side of Petrolon with the power stone. *(*JODY *picks up stone, climbs over vol-*

cano, and walks offstage. Curtain. Spaceship can be seen above the stage while the same music used before Act II can be heard.)

* * * * *

ACT III

Curtain opens on bright side of the planet. JODY, ERALK, ZORP, *and* TWERP *are onstage. The power stone is also sitting on stage. The music stops.*

ERALK: Jody from Earth, you have saved us. Now that we have our power stone back, our planet will become warm and beautiful again. The monsters will disappear, and we will be free to cultivate our planet and live in peace. We would like to present you with this ring, which has a small piece of the stone in it. It will remind you of your journey. We thank you. *(Hands ring to* JODY)

ZORP: Elernotweep!

TWERP: Fop dauwww!

ERALK: Zorp and Twerp say that you have done a magnificent job, and ask how we can repay you.

JODY: You've already given me this beautiful ring. And if you don't mind, Eralk, I should be getting back to Earth. My parents will be worried about me. I'm homesick.

ERALK: I understand completely. And do not worry; only a few hours have passed on Earth. You will be home before your parents miss you. We have recharged the ship for your return journey. I do not know how you came here or who sent you, but if it was a joke it was a good one. Thank you again. *(All say goodbye. Petrolonese wave.* JODY *exits, waving. Curtain closes. Spaceship appears above stage. The music played at the beginning can be heard. It is turned down to a very low volume, as spaceship disappears and* JODY *pops up in front of the curtain, asleep.)*

NARRATOR: Jody was home in time for breakfast.

VOICE OF MOTHER *(From offstage):* Jody, dear, time to wake up!

JODY *(Excitedly):* Oh, Mom! I've got to tell you about my dream. *(*JODY *stands, looks down at ring.)* Oh, but look at this ring! It wasn't a dream! *(Running offstage)* Mom! Mom!

NARRATOR: You have heard the amazing yet true story of how Jody saved the Petrolonese from the Terrastadon . . . with a little help from you. *(Music briefly gets louder.)* The End! *(Music fades.)*

Production Notes
JODY'S JOURNEY

Puppets

Jody

Jody is best made with a papier-mâché head and cloth body. She wears pajamas or nightgown.

The Petrolonese

Zorp, Twerp, and Eralk may be made with papier-mâché heads and cloth bodies, or all of cloth. They may also be made as glove puppets by decorating a work glove with eyes and other features and attaching a long tube at the base of the glove to cover the puppeteer's arm.

Since no one knows for sure what a person from Petrolon looks like, you have great flexibility in creating these puppets. If you are using papier-mâché heads, you may choose to paint them an unusual color, adding silver or other glitter for eyes. They may be bald, or have wild hair—use your imagination!

Zorp and Twerp may look more or less the same, but Eralk should stand out in some way from both of them.

Snatrons

The Snatrons can be made as all cloth puppets or as glove puppets, as described above; however, if Zorp, Twerp, and Eralk are glove puppets, the Snatrons should be cloth, and vice versa.

It's a good idea to make the Snatrons smaller than the other puppets in the play—their small size will add some variety to the show. Also, bold colors, such as orange or electric blue, will help these puppets stand out well against the dark background of Act II.

Terrastadon

There are many different ways to make the Terrastadon puppet. Use Eralk's description as a guide: "The Terrastadon has many arms, and many ears. . . . And even worse than his arms, with their claws and suction cups, is his gruesome mouth, which shoots poison!"

The most important feature is the poison-shooting mouth. I suggest using a small squirt gun filled with water immediately before the performance. The effect of squirting water is very exciting to an audience of children, particularly if this play is performed outside on a sunny day.

The simplest way to make a Terrastadon is to use a very big sponge of any shape or color. Cut a hole through it for the water gun and the puppeteer's hand. The water gun should be carefully inserted into the sponge so that it is hidden except for the tip of the nozzle. The puppeteer will hold up the puppet and squirt "poison" with his or her hand holding the water gun. To hide the puppeteer's arm, attach a colorful tube of fabric.

Decorate the sponge with eyes, ears, or whatever else you wish. This Terrastadon will not have a movable mouth, but it will be lightweight, and will require only one hand to operate.

You may create a more complicated Terrastadon out of a shower cap or plastic shopping bag. Cut an oval out of posterboard about the size of the puppeteer's hand. Then, cut the oval in half—these will be the upper and lower jaws. Cover them with plastic wrap or aluminum foil to make them water-resistant. On the top of the shower cap (and the outside), paste the two pieces approximately one inch apart, so that the straight edges are toward the inside. Check to make sure that the puppeteer can put his thumb below and fingers above the ovals to move the mouth when the Terrastadon speaks.

Very carefully, make a hole between the jaws large enough for the tip of the squirt gun to poke through. Reinforce the hole, stitching all around it with strong thread.

Complete the puppet with arms made of brightly colored plastic, metal tubes, or pipe cleaners. Attach the arms without puncturing the shower cap. Small pieces of sponge or rubber can be attached to the ends of the arms, and if you'd like, make big ears or antennae.

Attach a vibrantly colored wide cloth tube at the base of the shower cap. Make sure the stitching attaches the two firmly. The tube should be large enough to hide both of the puppeteer's arms, because one will be needed to operate the squirt gun and the other to support the puppet and operate his mouth when he speaks. Shower caps rip easily, so the Terrastadon should be operated with care. The puppeteer should allow ample time to put on and take off the puppet during the performance.

Sets

Bright Side of Petrolon

As with the puppets in this play, the sets can be made in a variety of ways. Explore the possibilities that excite you. Perhaps the bright side of Petrolon has many moons, stars, or suns on it. It may be painted in pastels or vibrant colors—pinks, greens, red, or violet— and have unusual plants and flowers growing. There may be many clouds in the sky.

Dangerous Side of Petrolon

The Terrastadon's side of the planet should be fairly dark and barren. It may be covered with little craters or volcanoes. Eyes may peep from the shadows. Various beasts may be pictured. It may be a gray, brown, or orange desert.

Props

Magic wand

A magic wand can easily be made from a rounded or pointed piece of posterboard, colored with markers and decorated with glitter or gold ribbon. It should be a convenient size and shape for Jody and the Petrolonese to hold in their hands. You will probably want to have at least two on hand, in case one is dropped during the performance.

Spaceship

Because the spaceship flies over the top of the puppet theater and not onstage, it may be fairly large—almost as big as the stage, if you like. Make it out of posterboard, in any color and shape you wish. It may have windows or lights, be saucer-shaped, or look like the space shuttle. Attach it to a long pole so that it can be lifted over the stage and be completely visible to the audience; a broom pole, pool cue, or classroom pointer would work well.

If you are performing in a darkened room, you may project a picture of a spaceship on the wall or a screen above the stage, using an overhead projector. Place the picture of the spaceship on the glass of the projector at the beginning of the performance; when Jody is traveling in the spaceship, the director of the play or someone else who knows the play well should turn on the projector, and move the picture in circles to make it appear as if the spaceship is flying. If there is room and the cord is long enough, the whole projector can even be pushed from side to side, to make the spaceship fly back and forth above the stage. When the scene change is over, the projector can be turned off to make the spaceship disappear.

Volcano

The volcano must be able to withstand Jody's "climbing" over it, so I recommend using corrugated cardboard rather than posterboard. Cut out a volcano shape and paint it. You might want to paste on strips of aluminum foil or colored paper to represent dried lava. Mount the volcano on a rod, and set several thumbtacks or nails below the bottom edge of the stage so that the rod may rest securely on them. (See diagram I.6.) For even greater stability, you might make the volcano out of two layers of thin wood attached only at the top. Spread the pieces apart at the bottom and clamp them around the edge of the stage.

Power stone

A real stone may be used, but you can easily make a lightweight stone that can be attached to the stage with Velcro. Shape aluminum foil until it is the desired shape and size, or wrap aluminum foil or wrapping paper around a wadded paper towel. Make at least two identical power stones, in case one is dropped or falls off the stage during the performance.

Ring

You may use an inexpensive ring, or make one out of 24-gauge or other lightweight wire. Be sure the stone in it resembles your power stone. Keep at least one more ring ready backstage, because it is an easy prop for a puppet to drop accidentally.

Roland and Celia

❖❖ **Roland and Celia**

A play with special underwater effects

Cast:
> ROLAND
> BIG FISH
> MAMA TURTLE
> WALRUS
> CELIA, *an octopus*
> STEINLEY, *a starfish*
> PHOSSIE, *a phosphorescent squid*
> NARRATOR

Sets:
> *Coral reef*
> *Deep part of the ocean*
> *Octopus' garden*

Props:
> *Seaweed*
> *Table with food on it*

ACT I

Introductory music plays briefly and is turned off.

NARRATOR: Welcome to our puppet show, *Roland and Celia*. This story takes place far away in a very deep, very blue ocean. Close your eyes and imagine yourselves beneath the waves. You are listening to the whales, who are singing messages to one another. *(Pauses for several seconds.*

117

Whale sounds are heard in background. Bubbles are blown up or outward from backstage, preferably by at least two people.) All around you, seahorses and colorful fish of all sizes are swimming, making bubbles and ripples in the clear water. You are swimming with them in and around the beautiful pink, red, and white coral—some of it shaped like mushrooms, fans, flowers, and feathery plumes.

The coral reef where you are swimming is the home of one of our heroes, a small turtle named Roland. *(Curtain opens on coral reef.* ROLAND *is onstage.)*

Roland swims around on the reef, admiring the plants and fish. He tries to make friends with some of the other creatures, but they think they are too grown up to play with him, and some don't even come near him when he speaks. *(Bubbles and whale sounds stop.* BIG FISH *appears on the corner of the stage.* ROLAND *looks up at him.)*

ROLAND: Good morning, Big Fish. Do you have time to play with me?

BIG FISH: Goodness, no. I have work to do. Just wait until *you're* grown up.

ROLAND *(Wistfully; watching him exit):* Goodbye! *(*MAMA TURTLE *appears on stage.)* Oh, hi, Mama. Will you play leapfrog with me?

MAMA TURTLE: Definitely not, dear, I'm much too busy. I'm just stopping to remind you never ever to go down to the deep part of the ocean. There are all sorts of animals who will chase you and try to eat you up. Worst of all, we know for a fact that there is an octopus who lives there, and you know how dangerous octopuses are.

ROLAND: Well, everyone always tells me they are the worst creatures in the ocean. Have you ever met one?

MAMA TURTLE *(Shocked):* Of course not. Don't you know there is no such thing as a good octopus? They are all wicked, hideous creatures that live in the dark. They are so stupid, they don't know how to talk or to do anything but hunt innocent creatures, spit poison at them, and who knows what after that.

So, remember, do not go into the deep, because if you meet an octopus, you will be very sorry. *(*MAMA TURTLE *swims away.)*

ROLAND: I hope I never meet that octopus down there. *(Brief pause)* Now, what shall I do today? No one ever wants to play leapfrog or any other kind of game. They all just swim around up there, eating. *(He sighs.)* Well, at least I can sing. *(Part of a popular song can be heard, while* ROLAND *appears to be singing it himself. He also swims and dances around. While he is singing, bubbles can be blown upward or outward from backstage.* ROLAND *exits. Curtain closes.)*

NARRATOR: Day after day, the same thing happened. Roland looked for playmates, but everyone else was too busy. Again and again, Roland heard warnings about the deep dark part of the ocean. One day, however, he decided he wanted to see it. It may be dangerous, he thought, but it may be exciting. Who knows what's really down there? *(Scary music is heard in background.)* And away he swam—down, down, down, farther and farther away from the coral reef and the light, toward the bottom of the ocean. *(Music continues while the set is changed.)*

*   *   *   *   *

ACT II

Curtain opens on the deep part of the ocean. A clump of seaweed hangs from above at one side of the mainstage. ROLAND *enters. The music fades out.*

ROLAND: Brrr! It sure is cold down here—and quiet. Maybe I shouldn't have come. I feel eyes staring out at me from behind every rock. I wonder if there really are monsters down here? *(A big splash is heard.)* What was that? *(Short pause while* WALRUS *appears in side window. Chase scene music begins.)*

WALRUS: Mmm! Turtle soup! *(*WALRUS *swims onto mainstage.)*

ROLAND *(Seeing* WALRUS*):* Oh, no! Help!

WALRUS *(Laughing):* You silly green turtle. I can swim faster than you, and I am going to catch you and eat you up!

ROLAND: Help! Mama! Big Fish! *(*WALRUS *laughs some more.)* I'll never be able to outswim him. Look, some seaweed! I'll hide in it and hope that he doesn't see me. *(*ROLAND *hides behind seaweed.)*

WALRUS: Where are you, rock climber? *(Looks around)* I guess he got away—this time. *(Gasping for breath a little)* I have to go up for air. *(*WALRUS *disappears.* ROLAND *breathes a sigh of relief.)*

ROLAND *(In trembling voice):* Oh, I'm so scared I can hear my heart pounding! I'm lucky I found this seaweed. Mama was right about this part of the ocean. I am going to go home right now, and I'll never come back again. *(He tries to wriggle loose of the seaweed, but cannot free himself.)* Oh, no, I can't get out! What am I going to do? *(*ROLAND

119

wriggles some more. At the same time, CELIA *appears.* ROLAND *screams.)*

CELIA: What's that? *(Sees* ROLAND*)* Oh, it's a little turtle caught in some seaweed. *(*CELIA *swims closer to* ROLAND.*)* Hello.

ROLAND *(Trembling):* Please don't shoot poison at me and eat me!

CELIA *(Amused):* Oh, I don't eat turtles. And I would never shoot poison. Sometimes I shoot out an inky smoke screen, but that is just to hide from things that chase me. Here, let me untangle you from this seaweed. *(*CELIA *untangles* ROLAND, *who is trembling still and eager to get away.)*

ROLAND: Thank you very much, Octopus. Please let me go home now.

CELIA: Why is everyone so scared of me? Whenever I try to meet someone, he swims away.

ROLAND: Well, everyone has always told me that you're very dangerous.

CELIA *(Upset):* But, that's not true and not fair! No one has ever even met me. What else have they told you?

ROLAND: That you're stupid and can't speak.

CELIA *(In challenging tone):* Well?

ROLAND: Well, I guess they were wrong about that. *(Pause)* And, they said that you're ugly.

CELIA: And what do you think?

ROLAND: Now that I see you up close, I don't think you're ugly at all. In fact, you're pretty.

CELIA: Thank you. I can change colors, too. I can become yellow or gray, brown or blue-green.

ROLAND *(Impressed):* Wow!

CELIA: And I have the most wonderful garden! Even though it is deep beneath the ocean, it is bright and really pretty. Would you like to come see it? There's no reason to be afraid.

ROLAND: I'd love to *(Pause)*, but what if more walruses come down?

CELIA: I'll make a smoke screen, and we can both escape.

ROLAND: O.K. Let's go! *(*ROLAND *and* CELIA *swim offstage. Curtain closes. During scene change, music to the Beatles' "Octopus' Garden" is heard. If there is enough time while the following lines are spoken,* ROLAND *and* CELIA *can appear together, swimming downward, in a side window.)*

NARRATOR: So the turtle and the octopus swam toward the octopus' garden. On the way, Roland asked her:

ROLAND *(Offstage):* What's your name?

CELIA *(Offstage):* Celia. What's yours?

ROLAND *(Offstage):* Roland.

NARRATOR: The two talked and talked. Even in the short time it took them to reach the octopus' garden, they learned quite a bit about each other.

* * * * *

ACT III

Curtain opens on garden set. ROLAND *and* CELIA *swim onstage.*
ROLAND *looks around in awe. The music remains on, but is turned down.*

ROLAND *(Awestruck):* Your garden is beautiful!

CELIA: Thank you. Would you like something to eat?

ROLAND: Oh, yes, I'm hungry!

CELIA *(Calling offstage):* Steinly! Could you bring us some food, please? (STEINLY *enters, carrying a table laid with a feast.* ROLAND *gasps.* CELIA *addresses* STEINLY.) Would you like to stay for dinner, Steinly? (STEINLY *disappears.* CELIA *laughs.*) He's so shy! Maybe he'll feel more comfortable the next time you come. Now, help yourself to dinner. (ROLAND *and* CELIA *eat for several seconds.*)

ROLAND: Mmm. That was great! Thank you very much, Celia.

CELIA: You're welcome, Roland. Would you like anything else?

ROLAND: No, thanks. I just want to look at these flowers and corals, unless . . . *(While the next few lines are spoken,* STEINLY *reappears and takes away table.)*

CELIA: Unless what?

ROLAND: Unless you want to play a game.

CELIA: Oh, I'd love to. How about leapfrog?

ROLAND: That's my favorite! *(Music is turned up.* ROLAND *and* CELIA *play leapfrog for ten or fifteen seconds. Then,* PHOSSIE *appears and the music stops.)*

CELIA: Hey, Phossie! Want to play?

PHOSSIE: No, thank you. I'm on my way to a concert. Would you and your friend care to join me?

ROLAND *(Without hesitation):* I'd love to! I've never been to a concert before. My name's Roland.

PHOSSIE: And you, Celia? Would *you* like to come? The Sea-Bottom Choir is singing.

CELIA: Oh, yes. Let's go! *(Short pause)* But wait, we can hear them from here. *(Choir music can be heard, very faintly at first, then growing louder.* ROLAND, CELIA, *and* PHOSSIE *listen together, happily dancing and waving their limbs to the music. The curtain closes. After a short pause,* ROLAND *and* CELIA *appear in separate side windows, swimming upward. Meanwhile, music is turned down and* NARRATOR *speaks.)*

NARRATOR: After the concert, Roland wanted to swim back up to the coral reef. He had so much to tell everyone there about what octopuses were really like. Celia escorted him to protect him and show him the way. From then on, the two were best friends. Celia would visit Roland on the coral reef and Roland would visit her in her garden. Celia and Roland were never too busy for each other. *(Curtain opens.* ROLAND *and* CELIA *appear onstage.)* They both joined the Sea-Bottom Choir, and then whales and fish from the coral reef joined. All together, they formed the Whole-Ocean Choristers—if you listen closely, you can hear them singing on windless nights. *(Choir music is turned up again, as all characters appear on stage. They sing and then swim out one by one, leaving just* ROLAND *and* CELIA.)*

ROLAND and CELIA *(As they swim off together and the curtain closes):* The End.

Production Notes
ROLAND AND CELIA

Puppets

Roland and Mama Turtle

A turtle puppet is fairly difficult to make, so you may choose to buy one; but if you'd like the challenge of making your own, here's one way of doing it:

Make the turtle's shell out of two oval pieces of green cloth stuffed with nylon or other light material. Since the finished shell will have a hump at the top but be flat on the bottom, the top piece should be larger than the bottom piece, so that the space between the two can be filled with stuffing. The bottom of Roland's shell should measure about five inches long by four inches wide; the bottom of Mama Turtle's shell should be about seven inches by six inches.

Sew the edges of the two pieces about three-quarters of the way around, stuff the shell, then finish sewing. If you wish, you may draw markings on the top with a fabric pen.

For the underside of the turtle, use fabric at least a quarter inch thick; quilted fabric works well. Place the shell on top of the fabric, and trace around the bottom. Cut out the traced piece and reinforce the edges, if necessary.

The head and body can be made out of a green sock. Follow the instructions in Chapter 2 for making a sock puppet with movable arms. Paste little eyes near the toe of the sock, and red felt or cloth for the mouth.

The next step is to sew the underside onto the bottom of the turtle's body (the body—the puppeteer's arm—will be placed *between* the underside and the shell). You needn't sew a large area together, but only attach a small section of the body to the center of the underside. Most of the puppeteer's hand should protrude in front.

Now, you will need to sew the top shell and underside together while someone is wearing the puppet's body, making sure the puppeteer will have enough room and flexibility to be able to hide the turtle's head between the shell and underside. Bend the underside to meet the shell, and sew the edges together with strong thread. Of course, the parts (front and back) where the puppeteer's hand and arm protrude should be left unsewn.

You have made a turtle!

Big Fish, Steinly, and Phossie

You can buy oven mitts in the shape of fish, or make fish puppets out of regular long oven mitts decorated with eyes and gills.

Big Fish, Steinly, and Phossie can also be made as simple rod puppets. Draw the appropriate shapes on colored posterboard, including eyes, gills, and any other markings you wish (add glitter for Phossie). Cut out each drawing, and tape a dowel rod, paint brush, or twig at a 45-degree angle on the back of each. For Steinly the starfish, make sure the rod is hidden behind one of the "arms"; the puppeteer must also take special care to keep his hand and the rod out of the sight of the audience during the show.

Another option in making Phossie is to begin by buying a sparkler or wand at the toy store. (These items are like flashlights with many fiber optic tubes at the end. When the light is turned on, the tubes light up to show sparkles inside.) Make a tube of brightly colored cloth long enough to extend from the tip of your fingers to the elbow. Put the tube around the fiber optic toy and securely attach one end of it just below the fibers. Paste two big eyes on the tube near the fibers. The puppeteer operating Phossie will grasp the toy under the tube, and turn the switch on immediately before Phossie's entrance.

Walrus

Buy a long oven mitt in brown, silver, gray, or black. Paste eyes, nose, and whiskers at the top of the mitt to make the face. When operating the walrus puppet, make him dart up and down as he swims, simulating the movement of a real walrus.

Celia

If you wish to have Celia closely resemble a real octopus, it will be helpful to consult a book with photographs first. On the other hand, there is plenty of room for whimsy in constructing an octopus puppet. Begin by stitching a shower cap of any color to a colored cloth tube long enough to hide the puppeteer's arm.

To define the puppet's mouth, cut two identical half ovals of posterboard to make the upper and lower mouth parts. On the top of the shower cap, paste the two parts approximately a half-inch apart, with straight edges facing. Now, reach inside the cap and check to make sure that the puppeteer can put his thumb below and fingers above the mouth parts to move it when Celia is speaking. Attach a piece of wide tape inside the cap to reinforce the shape of the gathered mouth.

Complete the puppet with eight arms made of stuffed colorful fabric or brightly colored plastic tubes. Tubes can be glued or taped to the shower cap. Stuffed arms should be sewn onto the tube of fabric directly below the seam where the shower cap and fabric are joined. Remember to operate this puppet with care, because shower caps rip easily.

A sturdier puppet can be made by using a toaster cover or cloth sack in place of the shower cap.

Sets

Coral reef

The narrator's description of Roland's home in Act I, along with any photographs you can find, may guide you in your illustrations. I suggest using a light blue or green background for the reef. Decorate it with coral of various shapes, and small fish with bubbles coming out of their mouths. Keep the colors simple—for example, soft oranges and pinks. The coral reef should be pretty, but not as spectacular as Celia's garden.

Deep part of the ocean

Dark posterboard is best for the background of the scary depths. Against it, you may use white or gray paint to outline stones, funnels, or caves. You may also paste pairs of eyes here and there, peering out of the darkness.

Octopus' garden

Celia's garden will look best against a bright background, such as yellow. Let your imagination guide you as you paint all kinds of fantastic underwater flowers, sponges, and corals. Nestle blue or other colored starfish among tall, supple weeds or stems, or paint them in the upper part of the set above the garden. You may paint a seahorse or two as well, and possibly a sand dollar on the garden floor. Try to use as many vibrant colors as possible.

Props

Seaweed

Use colored shredded plastic, paper, or yarn. Bind a large bunch of the "seaweed," top and bottom, with pieces of string. The bunch should be a little longer than the height of the puppet stage. Attach a loop of string at the very top, and hang the seaweed on a nail or knob above the stage before the beginning of Act II. Do not forget to remove it before Act III.

Table with food

Draw an oval table with a single center leg on white posterboard. Use markers or paint and a small brush to draw food on the table, laid out in a colorful array. Cut out the table and food. Then tape a dowel rod, paint brush, or stick onto the back of it, so that it can be carried on and offstage.

Notes on Performing

Movement of puppets

It can be great fun to make the puppets in this play enter and exit and move about onstage largely because the action takes place under water. Therefore, the puppets can swim onto the stage from high up or underneath, and they can swim around the stage without having to appear to "stand" on the bottom edge, as puppets usually do.

Act III

Act III can work very well with happy music being played throughout most of the scene, as suggested in the script. When Roland eats, he may move his front legs, as though swimming, to raise himself to the part of the table with the food on it. When playing leapfrog, Celia and Roland should take turns jumping or swimming over each other. Obviously, the puppets cannot really jump completely over one another, because they are always operated by puppeteers who are sitting below the stage. However, the effect can be simulated when the puppet who is leaping is held closer to the inside of the stage.